LEAH SCHAPIRA

Fresh & Easy
KOSHER COOKING

ORDINARY INGREDIENTS
EXTRAORDINARY MEALS

PHOTOGRAPHY   Dan Engongoro
DESIGN   RachelAdlerDesign.com
PUBLISHER   Mesorah Publications, ltd.

Published by ARTSCROLL / SHAAR PRESS

4401 Second Avenue / Brooklyn, NY 11232 / (718) 921-9000
www.artscroll.com

Distributed in Israel by SIFRIATI / A. GITLER
6 Hayarkon Street / Bnei Brak 51127 / Israel

Distributed in Europe by LEHMANNS
Unit E, Viking Business Park, Rolling Mill Road
Jarrow, Tyne and Wear, NE32 3DP / England

Distributed in Australia and New Zealand by GOLDS WORLD OF JUDAICA
3-13 William Street / Balaclava, Melbourne 3183, Victoria / Australia

Distributed in South Africa by KOLLEL BOOKSHOP
Ivy Common / 105 William Road / Norwood 2192 / Johannesburg, South Africa

ISBN-10: 1-4226-1144-2 / ISBN-13: 978-1-4226-1144-9

Printed in the USA by Noble Book Press

WHY I COOK

Those who knew me when I was a little girl remember that I was the pickiest eater ever. It wasn't the food — there was always delicious food and plenty of amazing cooks. While everyone else enjoyed the meals, I turned up my nose. There were, however, some foods I enjoyed. At three, I entered a tangerine phase. At five, I ate pizza three times a day. On the rare occasion that I'd eat something else, the foods couldn't touch: chicken on one side of the plate, fries on the other. If they touched, my meal was over.

My parents ignored, promised, and pleaded. They took me to doctors. Finally, when I was eight years old, my mother took me into the kitchen. She involved me in the preparations—if I saw everything that went into a dish, I wouldn't be scared to try it. She showed me how to make French fries. If I liked fries, why shouldn't I like other dishes with the same ingredients? I became obsessed with knowing how everything was prepared. Once I made dishes, I wanted to try them. As a teenager, I took cookbooks to bed and fell asleep reading recipes.

To all mothers of picky eaters: Never force children to eat. Instead, teach them to cook. Let them understand how food is prepared. Learn what appeals to them. If they love BBQ potato chips, start incorporating the taste into other foods. There's a world of great flavors out there.

ABOUT THIS BOOK

This cookbook is all about easy, uncomplicated recipes for every day or for occasions. Some are family favorites and some are new additions that will become your family favorites. I like to use ingredients from my pantry, adding new twists and improving techniques. I hope that this cookbook will keep cooking from turning into a chore. Since we're going to cook, we might as well enjoy it!

You'll find menu suggestions and ideas in the first pages of the book. The photos will help you decide if you want to check out a particular recipe. These thumbnails are not meant to be a complete guide, but are a helpful aid as you plan your meals.

Many main dish recipes are accompanied by "Goes With" photos and page references. "Goes With's" are only suggestions, usually a side dish and sometimes a soup or a salad.

A few more points before we start cooking: Each pot and stove heat food differently. As always, trust your instincts. If it doesn't look ready, cook a bit longer. Salt is the most important seasoning when it comes to cooking and should usually not be skipped. However, taste is a personal preference and your food should be seasoned to your taste or to suit your dietary needs. I use sea salt or table salt for all my cooking. If you do use kosher salt, adjust the amount listed in the ingredient column.

In 2010, I co-founded www.cookkosher.com, a kosher recipe community where you, the cook, can contribute your own recipes and explore recipes from other kosher food lovers. Head over there to discover and share a world of food created by home cooks just like you.

Have fun, get creative, add some spice to your everyday meals, and let the cooking begin.

CONTENTS

BRUNCH & LUNCH

MAIN DISHES

KITCHEN
INFORMATION GUIDE

ACKNOWLEDGMENTS

First and foremost, I acknowledge very gratefully the *hashgacha pratis* and the constant help and *berachah* from the **Ribbono Shel Olam**. Nothing could be done without His continual *siyata d'Shamaya*.

There's much more behind this cookbook than a girl and a mixing bowl. Each recipe on these pages involved the enthusiasm and support of family and friends, tasters and testers. I know that I can trace my way around the kitchen to **my dear grandmothers**. You are my biggest fans. To **my mother**, Mrs. Tilly Roth, and **my mother-in-law**, Mrs. Ricki Shapira. From my first step into the kitchen through your genuine support today, you've taught me and provided the example for me to aspire. To my sister-in-law **Devorah**, you were the first one to share your recipes and menus back in the day when we were both newlyweds. To my sister-in-law **Debbie**: When you made my shidduch did you realize you'll be a partner to food? To my sister, **Miriam**, you are my sounding board. Thanks for being the best listener and keeping me grounded. To

Sheva, Devorie, and **Bruchie** — It means so much to me to have so much support from all of you. You are always so excited to try each new recipe and I love to hear your opinions.

To **my husband, father, father-in-law, brothers,** and **brothers-in-law**. Thank you so much for helping me tweak and perfect by tasting and critiquing. Cooking for you has always been fun. You're also responsible for the dose of Torah that's included in this book, and I appreciate all of your insights.

To my sister and graphic designer, **Rachel Adler** of RADesign. You are brilliant! I feel so lucky to be able to work on a project like this with you. The graphics and cover design are a big part of the wow factor that makes this book so special -- to me and, I hope, to others as well.

To my friends **Chaya Friedman, Chaya Jacobowitz, Debbie Fertig,** and **Krassie Schon**: You are my sous chefs! At each photo shoot, you helped me prep, cut, cook, set up, clean up, and finally eat the food! To **Miriam Goldenberg**, you've always provided great advice. To all my neighbors old and new. Thanks for lending me props, sharing your recipes, and tasting the food.

I owe my biggest career leap to **Rechy Frankfurter** editor of Ami magazine. Thank you for always challenging me to bring my ideas to higher and higher levels. Thank you **Mr. Eli Paley** and **Nomee Shaingarten** of Mishpacha Magazine, for giving me room within your pages to grow. To my editor, **Victoria Dwek**, your writing and editing skills, combined with your enthusiasm and love of cooking, made you the ideal person with whom to work. **Mr. Dan Engongoro** — you are an amazing photographer, and I've learned so much from your technical and creative expertise over the past three years. It's because of you that all the food in these pages looks as good as it tastes.

Thanks to ArtScroll's senior editors **Felice Eisner** and **Judi Dick**, who urged me to provide answers on the nitty-gritty, size of pots and pans, and everything I assumed wasn't necessary. You completed this book and as they say — behind every great book is an amazing editor.

Thanks to **Tova Ovits,** who proofread diligently and kept us on our toes, and to **Devorah Bloch,** who ever so patiently fixed up page by page so that it looks as spectacular as it does.

Many thanks to **Gavriel Sanders,** whose marketing expertise is beyond compare.

Last but not least, the biggest thank-you belongs to **Rabbi Meir Zlotowitz** and **Rabbi Gedaliah Zlotowitz** who believed in this book and in my ability to reach the reading and cooking public.

APPETIZER IDEAS

PESACH MENU

SUBSTITUTE EQUAL AMOUNTS OF POTATO STARCH FOR THE FLOUR

88 | Caramelized Shallots

98 | Breakfast Home Fries

238 | Overnight Potato Kugel

232 | Egg & Liver Tower

92 | Squash Soufflés

208 | Orange-Glazed Flanken

210 | Beef With Caramelized Pearl Onions

192 | Chicken Fajitas

290 | Hot Chocolate Molten Cake

324 | Tri-Color Fruit Purée

308 | Watermelon Sorbet

300 | Cheese Roulade

304 | Breakfast Cheesecake

322 | Chocolate Mousse With Pear Chips

MAKE-IN TAKE-OUT

QUICK & EASY

44 | Mediterranean Tomato Salad

50 | Guacamole With Tortilla Crisps

138 | Baked Basil Fries

272 | Jam Pie

112 | Honey-Mustard Couscous

152 | Garlic Knots

220 | Teriyaki Salmon Skewers

192 | Chicken Fajitas

194 | Basil Chicken Wraps

166 | Honey-Mustard Chicken

176 | Chicken Stir Fry

FREEZES WELL

WHAT'S IN SEASON: FALL AND WINTER

The earth certainly knows the ideal time for the hearty produce of fall and winter. Lucky for us, apples are at their peak right around Rosh Hashanah time. Pomegranates are also plentiful then — but don't shop early. Summer pomegranates, shipped from the southern hemisphere, will likely be expensive. Winter produce also translates into amazingly rich soups. You might have a tad smaller selection, but fall and winter produce still offer lots of flavor and nutrition.

FALL

Apples • Broccoli • Cabbage • Chestnuts Cauliflower • Celery Root • Coconuts • Dates Fennel • Figs • Garlic • Grapes • Leeks Mushrooms • Onions • Oranges • Papayas Pears • Peppers • Pomegranates • Pumpkins Radishes • Squash • Tangerines

WINTER

Bananas • Broccoli • Cabbage • Celery Root Chestnuts • Citrus fruits • Clementines • Cranberries • Grapefruits • Kiwi Fruit • Kohlrabi • Leeks Oranges • Parsnip • Passion Fruit • Pineapple Potatoes • Rosemary • Squash • Sweet Potatoes Tangerines • Tropical Fruits • Yams

SOUPS

CARROT & CILANTRO SOUP

YIELD 6 SERVINGS

1	**LARGE ONION,** DICED
10	**LARGE CARROTS,** PEELED AND CUT INTO CHUNKS
2 TBSP	**OIL**
6 CUPS	**WATER,** IF NEEDED
1 TBSP	**CHICKEN-FLAVORED CONSOMMÉ POWDER**
½ TSP	**SALT**
¼ TSP	**PEPPER**
1 BUNCH	**CILANTRO**
•	**TOASTED PINE NUTS,** FOR GARNISH

Cilantro is an herb with wide lacy green leaves. The seeds of a cilantro plant are known as coriander. In some countries, cilantro is referred to as coriander leaves. Cilantro looks similar to parsley, but has a more pungent aroma. If you don't like cilantro, you can substitute parsley.

1 In a 6-quart pot, place the onion, carrots, oil, and seasoning. Fill the pot ¾ full with water. Insert the cilantro in a mesh bag or place it right on top. Bring water to a boil. Lower heat and cook, slightly uncovered, for 1 hour. Let cool.

2 Remove and discard the cilantro. Blend the soup with an immersion blender. Reheat and serve warm. Garnish with pine nuts.

FRENCH ONION SOUP

YIELD 4 SERVINGS

3-4 TBSP	**OIL** OR **BUTTER**
3	**LARGE ONIONS,** THINLY SLICED
1½ TBSP	**FLOUR**
4 TBSP	**ONION SOUP MIX**
6 CUPS	**BOILING WATER**
1	**BAY LEAF**
¼ CUP	**RED WINE**
•	**BAGUETTES,** OPTIONAL
•	**MOZZARELLA CHEESE,** OPTIONAL

My editor and I argued about this recipe. She claimed, "You cannot substitute oil for butter in French Onion Soup! It just won't taste the same. It won't have that sweetness."

I replied, "But what if they want to make the soup for a meat meal?"

She also questioned my use of onion soup mix. "What about the beef consommé?"

"Yes," I agreed, "that's really the right ingredient — I just thought that most people wouldn't have beef consommé cubes in their pantries. They have onion soup mix."

"So, they'll buy beef cubes," she replied. She told me she makes onion soup every week and buys parve Telma beef cubes by the dozen.

Lastly, she didn't think that it was practical that every recipe for French Onion Soup includes the step of ladling the soup into ovenproof bowls, inserting the bread and cheese, and then baking in an oven. "Who owns oven-proof bowls?" she asked me.

"I do!" I told her, "And so do my mother and my aunt and my sister..."

She offered another option: "About ten minutes before serving, I pour croutons into the soup, covering the top. Then, I layer slices of cheese on top of the croutons, leaving the soup over low heat. Some of the cheese melts into the soup, making it creamier. The rest melts on top of the croutons. Then, with a large ladle, I scoop up the soup along with a nice layer of croutons and melted cheese."

1 Heat the oil in a 6-quart pot over high heat. Add onions. Cook for 10 minutes, stirring occasionally, until browned. Add flour; mix well. Add onion soup mix and stir until thoroughly distributed. Add boiling water and bay leaf. Bring to a boil and cook for 10 minutes.

2 Add red wine, return to a boil, and cook for 5 minutes. Lower the heat, cover, and simmer for an additional 10-15 minutes. Remove bay leaf.

3 While soup is cooking, cut a French baguette into 8 slices on a diagonal and toast in oven for 5 minutes.

4 Ladle the soup into ovenproof bowls. Top each portion with 2 pieces of toasted baguette and sprinkle with grated cheese. Transfer the bowls to a cookie sheet and broil in oven until the cheese melts.

ROASTED GARLIC SOUP

PARVE

YIELD 4 SERVINGS

2 HEADS	GARLIC
1/3 CUP	OLIVE OIL
3 TBSP	FLOUR
4 1/2 CUPS	WATER
2 TSP	CHICKEN-FLAVORED CONSOMMÉ POWDER
1 CUP	EXTRA THIN EGG NOODLES, UNCOOKED
3-4 SPRIGS	PARSLEY, CHOPPED

When the Sages try to dissuade a person from sinning just because he is in a rut due to a previous sin, they compare the sinning to the strong scent of garlic: "If someone eats garlic, does that mean that he needs to continue eating garlic?"

Garlic's notorious scent is also featured in a story that illustrates Reb Chiya's sensitivity to his fellow man. Once while delivering a Torah lecture, Rebbe Yehudah HaNasi was greatly disturbed by the smell of garlic. He requested that the student who had eaten garlic leave the room. Reb Chiya realized that the one who smelled of garlic would be greatly embarrassed, and so he got up and left. He knew that once he left, the other person wouldn't be embarrassed and would also leave. After all, if the great Reb Chiya could admit to eating garlic, he too could do so.

The tried-and-true trick to enjoying garlic without the smell is to first eat a sprig of parsley. It's probably no coincidence that many garlic recipes contain parsley too.

1 Preheat oven to 350°F.

2 Without peeling them, slice the heads of garlic in half crosswise. Spread the oil on the bottom of a glass baking pan. Place the garlic halves cut side down in the pan.

3 Bake for 45 minutes to 1 hour. When ready, you'll be able to easily lift the peel off each garlic head, much like a hat.

4 Transfer peeled garlic to a 4-quart soup pot.

Top with flour. Using a potato masher, mash the flour and garlic until a smooth paste forms. Cook this mixture over low heat for 1-2 minutes, stirring constantly. Add water and consommé powder and stir.

5 Cover pot and cook for 20 minutes, stirring occasionally. Raise heat to medium, add the noodles, and continue cooking for 5-8 minutes until the noodles are cooked through. Sprinkle with chopped parsley.

CREAM OF LEEK SOUP

YIELD 3-4 SERVINGS

3	**LARGE LEEKS,** WHITE AND LIGHT GREEN PARTS ONLY
2-3 TBSP	**OIL**
1	**SMALL ONION,** DICED
4 TBSP	**FLOUR**
2 CUPS	**PARVE CHICKEN-FLAVORED STOCK**
¼ CUP	**WHITE WINE**
•	**SALT AND PEPPER,** TO TASTE
¾ CUP	**MILK**

Creamy soups are the ultimate winter comfort food. Leeks have a mild onion-like taste, so if you like onion soup and are ready for some fresh flavor, this soup is for you. You can create parve chicken-flavored stock by dissolving 2 teaspoons of chicken-flavored consommé powder in 2 cups of water.

1 Slice the white and light-green parts of the leek in half vertically. Wash well and cut crosswise into thin slices.

2 Heat the oil in a medium saucepan over medium heat. Add the leek and onion; sauté for 10 minutes, stirring occasionally, until translucent.

3 Add the flour to the pan, stirring constantly for 1-2 minutes. Add the stock and bring to a boil. Lower the heat. Add white wine, salt, and pepper and simmer for 10 minutes. Add the milk and heat thoroughly, taking care that the soup does not come to a boil.

JALAPEÑO & BROCCOLI SOUP

A broccoli soup with a slight kick. If you're not into spicy, just omit the jalapeño and you'll have a wonderful warm comfort soup. Make sure you wear gloves when deseeding the pepper, and avoid touching your eyes afterward.

Toasting the almonds with oil will give you crispy tasty almonds that are surprisingly so much better than toasting them plain. For that reason alone it's worth trying this recipe.

YIELD 6 SERVINGS

2	**LEEKS,** WHITE PART ONLY, DICED
1	**ONION,** DICED
2 TBSP	**OIL**
2 LB	**FROZEN BROCCOLI,** CUTS OR FLORETS
1 HEAPING TBSP	**CHICKEN-FLAVORED CONSOMMÉ POWDER**
1	**JALAPEÑO PEPPER,** DESEEDED, OPTIONAL
4 CUPS	**WATER**
•	**SALT AND PEPPER,** TO TASTE

GARNISH

¼ CUP	**SLICED ALMONDS**
3 TBSP	**OIL**

1 Sauté the diced leek and onion in a 4- or 5-quart pot. Add the broccoli and consommé powder and sauté for 5 minutes. Add the jalapeño pepper and add water just to cover.

2 Cover and cook over medium heat for 30 minutes. Blend with an immersion blender. Taste; season with salt and pepper to taste (you may not need salt at all).

3 Preheat oven to 450°F. Place the almonds into a baking pan. Drizzle with the oil. Bake for 5-7 minutes. Watch carefully as the almonds can quickly burn. Garnish each bowl with a few almonds.

ORZO BASIL CHICKEN SOUP

MEAT

When making a large pot of chicken soup for yom tov, I always find I'm left with lots of chicken broth while all the vegetables are gone. I either freeze the leftovers or make this soup from the broth. It's a new, fresh soup without the work. You can also shred any leftover soup chicken and add to the pot.

YIELD 6-8 SERVINGS

9 CUPS	**CHICKEN SOUP**
½–¾ CUP	**ORZO,** UNCOOKED
3 TBSP	**BASIL,** CHIFFONADE (SEE NOTE)
1½ CUPS	**COOKED CHICKEN,** SHREDDED
•	**SALT AND PEPPER,** TO TASTE

1 In a large stockpot, combine the chicken soup, orzo, basil, and chicken over high heat. Bring to a boil and cook until the orzo is cooked through, about 15 minutes.

2 Remove from heat and season with salt and pepper, as needed.

NOTE

To chiffonade is to cut any leaves into thin strips. Pile up a few basil leaves and roll them as you would a jellyroll. Using a sharp knife, cut into thin strips and separate into individual ribbons.

ROASTED TOMATO SOUP

YIELD 6 SERVINGS

2 LB	**TOMATOES** (ABOUT 4 BASEBALL-SIZED)
6 CLOVES	**GARLIC,** PEELED AND LEFT WHOLE
¼	**MEDIUM ONION**
2 TBSP	**OLIVE OIL**
1½ TBSP	**VINEGAR**
1 TBSP	**ITALIAN SEASONING** (OR ½ OREGANO, ½ BASIL)
•	**SALT AND PEPPER,** TO TASTE
1 TSP	**BROWN SUGAR**
1¾–2 CUPS	**CHICKEN STOCK,** HOT

The best thing about this soup is that you cook it in the oven. Dump it all together and forget about it. This is perfect for a lazy summer day, when tomatoes are at their sweetest.

1 Preheat oven to 375°F.

2 Line a 9x13-inch pan with parchment paper. Cut tomatoes into thirds and place in the pan. Add garlic cloves and onion. Drizzle with olive oil and vinegar. Season with Italian seasoning, salt, pepper, and brown sugar.

3 Roast for 45 minutes.

4 Transfer to a large bowl. Add hot chicken stock. Using an immersion blender, puree until soup is smooth. Taste and adjust seasonings.

ZUCCHINI & ASPARAGUS SOUP

YIELD 4 SERVINGS

2 TBSP	**OIL**
1	**LARGE ONION,** DICED
3 TBSP	**FLOUR**
2	**LARGE GREEN SQUASH,** CUT INTO CHUNKS WITH PEEL
2 16oz BAGS	**FROZEN CUT ASPARAGUS**
3-4 TBSP	**ONION SOUP MIX,** TO TASTE
5-8 CUPS	**WATER,** AS NEEDED
	SALT AND PEPPER, TO TASTE
	TOASTED PINE NUTS, FOR GARNISH, OPTIONAL

My friend Debbie is one of my toughest food critics. She lives next door, so whenever I experiment with something new, I send over a portion for her to taste. When she developed this soup, she sent some over for me to taste instead.

1 Heat the oil in a 6-quart pot over medium heat. Add the onion; cook until soft. Add flour and stir until combined. Add the squash chunks, 1 bag of frozen asparagus, and onion soup mix, and stir. Bring to a boil. Cook for 5 minutes, stirring occasionally. Cover with water and simmer for 20 minutes. Puree using an immersion blender.

2 Add the second bag of asparagus and 4-5 cups water. Return to a boil and simmer for an additional 20 minutes.

3 Garnish with toasted pine nuts, if desired.

SUMMER FRUIT SOUP

YIELD 8-10 SERVINGS

8 CUPS	**DARK RED PLUMS, PEACHES, APRICOTS AND/OR NECTARINES,** SLICED IN WEDGES, PEEL ON
1 CUP	**DARK RED CHERRIES,** PIT IN AND STEM REMOVED
1 CUP	**SUGAR**
5 CUPS	**WATER**
1½ TBSP	**CORNSTARCH**
1 TBSP	**VANILLA SUGAR**

In Israel, when peaches, plums, apricots, and nectarines are in season, you can't hide from the abundance. Grocery stores sell them in baskets, and it's often hard for a family to finish all the fruit before it is overripe. What do you do then? Some make a crisp or crumble, and others, like my sister-in-law Debbie, make soup.

1   In a 10-quart pot, combine fruit, sugar, and water. Bring to a boil. While it is boiling, remove 1 cup water; mix it with cornstarch. Return mixture to pot. Add vanilla sugar.

2   Cook 15 minutes over medium heat. Taste — the soup should be sweet. Add more sugar if necessary. Remove from heat. The soup should turn darker as time passes. Let cool and serve chilled.

ROASTED GARLIC & BUTTERNUT SQUASH SOUP

YIELD 6 SERVINGS

2	**LARGE BUTTERNUT SQUASH**
1 LARGE HEAD	**GARLIC,** TOP SLICED OFF
1	**LARGE SPANISH ONION,** DICED
2 TBSP	**OIL**
	WATER TO COVER
½ TSP	**SALT** + MORE TO TASTE
⅛ TSP	**BLACK PEPPER**
•	**FRESH PARSLEY,** TO GARNISH
•	**CROUTONS,** OPTIONAL

Butternut squash soup is a really popular easy winter soup. The hardest part of preparing it is peeling and de-seeding the rock-hard squash. When I first noticed butternut squash being sold in packages, all cut up and ready to cook, I wondered who would spend the extra money on that. After battling with a really difficult squash, I understood! I was just as ready as anyone else to run out and buy the pre-cubed version.

The roasting in this recipe adds an additional depth of flavor to the soup. The process brings out the natural sweetness in both the garlic and the squash and intensifies their natural flavors. It will also soften the squash, making it easier to work with later.

1 Preheat oven to 400°F. Line a baking sheet with parchment paper. Cut each squash in half and place cut side down on the baking sheet. Wrap the garlic in foil and place alongside the squash. Bake for 1 hour or until squash is soft.

2 Meanwhile, in a 5-quart pot, sauté onion in oil until golden.

3 Remove squash and garlic from oven. Allow to cool slightly scoop the pits out of the squash, peel, and add squash to the pot. Squeeze the garlic cloves from their peel and add to the pot. Add water just to cover (about 6 cups). Add the salt and pepper. Cook for 20-30 minutes. Blend well, using an immersion blender or food processor.

4 Adjust seasonings to taste and top with fresh parsley. Serve with croutons, if desired.

WHAT'S IN SEASON: SPRING AND SUMMER*

Take advantage of abundant spring and summer crops by planning your menus around in-season produce. Though many items shown here, such as tomatoes, can be found year-round nowadays, flavor is at its peak in the summertime. In-season locally grown produce is also much less expensive.

*Northern Hemisphere

SPRING

Asparagus • Avocados • Beets • Blueberries Cucumbers • Garlic • Lettuce • Mint • New Potatoes • Papayas • Peas • Radishes • Rhubarb • Scallions • Shallots • Snow Peas Strawberries • Sugar Snap Peas • Vidalia Onions • Zucchini

SUMMER

Apricots • Blueberries • Basil • Cantaloupe Celery • Cherries • Corn • Cucumbers Eggplant • Garlic • Grapes • Honeydew Mangoes • Nectarines • Peaches • Peppers Plums • Raspberries • Scallions • Shallots Squash • Tomatoes • Watermelon • Zucchini

SALADS

MRS. WEISS'S EGGPLANT SALAD

YIELD 4 CUPS

1	**LARGE EGGPLANT**
¼ CUP	**EXTRA LIGHT OLIVE OIL** OR **CANOLA OIL**
⅓ CUP	**WATER**
3 TBSP	**VINEGAR**
1 TSP	**CUMIN**
1	**RED BELL PEPPER,** DICED
1	**GREEN BELL PEPPER,** DICED
1 11oz CAN	**CORN,** DRAINED
¾ TBSP	**SALT**
3 CLOVES	**GARLIC,** PEELED AND CRUSHED

Every Shabbos, Mrs. Weiss's home is filled with guests who enjoy an abundant spread of dips and salads. It must be time-consuming, but her table has grown to be renowned. She also dabbles in shidduchim, pairing up a guest from last week with one who passed through her home the week before — so if you're in the market for good food or marriage, you might want to nab an invitation. This eggplant salad is one of the favorites on her table.

1   Preheat oven to 425°F.

2   Wash the eggplant well and remove the stem. Slice the eggplant in half lengthwise. Cut each half into ¾-inch thick strips and then dice. You want most pieces to have a bit of the peel.

3   Line a large baking sheet with parchment paper. Arrange the diced eggplant on the sheet and toss well with oil. Make sure that every piece of eggplant is coated with a bit of oil (add an additional Tablespoon of oil if necessary). Bake for 1 hour or until all the eggplant pieces are dark brown.

4   Transfer the eggplant to a bowl and add water, vinegar, and cumin. Add peppers and corn. Season with salt and garlic. Refrigerate overnight to allow the flavors to blend.

CUCUMBER SALAD

8	**SMALL PERSIAN CUCUMBERS,** THINLY SLICED
1	**RED ONION,** HALVED AND SLICED INTO THIN STRIPS
2 TSP	**CHOPPED DILL**
2 TSP	**OIL**
¾ CUP	**VINEGAR**
½ TBSP	**SALT**
2 TSP	**SUGAR**
¾ TSP	**BLACK PEPPER**

This is a staple on my mother-in-law's Shabbos table. You don't need a mandoline to slice the cucumbers thinly — simply prepare this ahead of time using a standard vegetable peeler. Although any cucumbers will do, the best for this salad are not kirbies or English cucumbers, but Persian cucumbers. Those that are smaller in size pack a better flavor. My mother-in-law substitutes a packet of Splenda for the sugar.

1 Combine cucumbers, onions, and dill.

2 Dress with oil, vinegar, salt, sugar, and black pepper. Toss to combine.

3 Chill until ready to serve.

MEDITERRANEAN TOMATO SALAD

YIELD 2 CUPS

3	**PLUM TOMATOES,** DICED
½	**SMALL RED ONION,** DICED
1½ TBSP	**DILL,** CHOPPED
4	**MUSHROOMS,** PEELED AND DICED
15	**BLACK OLIVES** PITTED AND SLICED
2 TBSP	**OLIVE OIL**
⅓ TSP	**SALT**
⅛ TSP	**BLACK PEPPER**
½ TSP	**ZA'ATAR**

What do tomato, zucchini, pumpkin, eggplant, sweet pepper, and cucumber have in common? I would guess that your first response would be that they are all vegetables, right? Wrong. They're actually fruits.

Botanically, scientists have a long explanation of what makes an item a fruit. In simple terms, if produce has seeds, it's technically a fruit. These "fruits" are treated as vegetables in cooking simply because they are not sweet. The word "vegetable" is a culinary term and has no scientific meaning. So, any "fruit" that we use and cook as a vegetable is still a vegetable.

In 1893, fruit importer Jon Nix sued New York customs collector Edward Hedden to recover duties he paid when importing tomatoes from the West Indies. At that time vegetables required a 10 percent tariff while fruits were imported duty free. When the case reached the United State Supreme Court, the justices ruled unanimously that a tomato is a vegetable.

1 In a medium bowl, combine the tomatoes, onion, dill, mushrooms, and black olives.

2 Dress with olive oil, salt, black pepper, and za'atar. Stir to combine.

NOTE

Za'atar is a mixture of herbs and spices with Middle Eastern origins. Generally, it includes ground thyme, oregano, and marjoram, with toasted sesame seeds. Some variations include savory, cumin, coriander, or fennel seeds.

You can also use za'atar to season meat and vegetables, or to sprinkle on your pizza. Mix it with olive oil, spread on bread dough, and bake.

NUTTY
CABBAGE SALAD

YIELD 4-5 CUPS

1 HEAD	**GREEN CABBAGE,** SHREDDED OR 32 oz BAGGED CABBAGE
1	**LARGE RED ONION,** SLICED
¼ CUP	**FRESH DILL,** CHOPPED (EQUIVALENT TO 1 3.4oz PKG)
6oz	**ROASTED SALTED SHELLED SUNFLOWER SEEDS**
4oz	**ROASTED SALTED SHELLED PUMPKIN SEEDS**

DRESSING

½ CUP	**MAYONNAISE**
¼ CUP	**SUGAR**
¼ CUP	**VINEGAR**
PINCH	**BLACK PEPPER**
•	**SALT,** TO TASTE

1 In a large salad bowl, toss together the cabbage, red onion, dill, and seeds. In a second bowl, thoroughly combine dressing ingredients.

2 Before serving, pour the dressing over the salad and toss. (Note: Because the salt in the seeds will vary depending on the brand, you must taste and adjust.)

LAYERED MUNG SALAD

YIELD 6 CUPS

2 CUPS	**MUNG** OR **BEAN SPROUTS**
2 CUPS	**CHERRY TOMATOES,** HALVED
7–9	**LARGE MUSHROOMS,** THINLY SLICED
1	**LEEK,** THINLY SLICED
1 15oz CAN	**BABY CORN,** DRAINED AND SLICED
3½ oz	**CASHEW NUTS**

DRESSING

2 TBSP	**SUGAR**
2 TBSP	**MAYONNAISE**
2 TBSP	**WATER**
1 TBSP	**VINEGAR**
•	**SALT AND PEPPER,** TO TASTE

1 Layer the salad ingredients in order, beginning with the bean sprouts on the bottom and ending with the cashews on top.

2 Combine the dressing ingredients. Toss right before serving.

ROASTED MUSHROOM & PEPPER SALAD

PARVE

1 Preheat oven to 400°F.

2 In a large roaster pan, arrange peppers and mushrooms. Drizzle with olive oil and soy sauce. Roast for 20 minutes.

3 To prepare dressing, combine ingredients. Toss with the hot vegetables. Serve warm or chilled.

YIELD 4 CUPS

2	**RED BELL PEPPERS,** CUT INTO STRIPS
2	**YELLOW** OR **ORANGE BELL PEPPERS,** CUT INTO STRIPS
4	**PORTOBELLO MUSHROOMS,** CUT INTO STRIPS
¼ CUP	**OIL**
2 TBSP	**SOY SAUCE**

DRESSING

¼ CUP	**SUGAR**
2 TBSP	**VINEGAR**
1 TBSP	**DIJON MUSTARD**
2	**SCALLIONS,** WHITE ONLY, THINLY SLICED
1 TBSP	**PARSLEY FLAKES**

NOTE

The pretty presentation of this salad when it is assembled in layers makes it a beautiful gift, whether for Purim or simply as a friendly gesture. A clear glass jar provides a neat, clean, and appetizing packaging idea. Make sure the jar has a wide mouth. Place dressing separately in a small container (or matching mini glass jar) so the salad doesn't spoil. Finally, tie a raffia ribbon and hang a tag with your warm wishes.

GUACAMOLE WITH TORTILLA CRISPS

PARVE

YIELD 6 SERVINGS

- 5 **10-INCH TORTILLA WRAPS**
- • **OIL,** FOR FRYING

GUACAMOLE

- 3 **RIPE AVOCADOS,** DICED
- 1 **MEDIUM SIZE TOMATO,** DICED
- 2 **SCALLIONS,** WHITE AND LIGHT GREEN PARTS ONLY, THINLY SLICED
- 3 TBSP **LEMON JUICE**
- ½ TSP **SALT** -
- PINCH **BLACK PEPPER**
- PINCH **CAYENNE PEPPER** OR **RED PEPPER FLAKES**

Tortilla Crisps can be cut or sliced into any shape, giving you an opportunity to be inventive next Chanukah or on any occasion. Draw a 4-inch dreidel shape on a piece of paper and cut out to make a stencil. Place the stencil on the tortilla and trace around the shape with a sharp knife. Repeat and follow instructions below for a fun touch to your festive meal.

1 Using a pizza cutter, cut tortilla wraps into trianglular wedges.

2 Heat oil in a small pot over high heat. When oil is hot, drop in a few tortilla wedges. The wedges should sizzle and puff up slightly in under a minute. Turn over. The second side will be done in a matter of seconds. Using a slotted spoon, remove from oil and drain on paper towels. Repeat with all wedges.

3 To prepare guacamole, combine all ingredients. Taste and adjust seasoning.

PARMESAN CITRUS SALAD

1 HEAD	**ROMAINE LETTUCE,** SHREDDED
2	**NAVEL ORANGES,** PEELED AND SLICED INTO ROUNDS
3	**SCALLIONS,** WHITE AND LIGHT GREEN PARTS ONLY, SLICED
1	**RIPE AVOCADO,** THINLY SLICED
½ CUP	**TOASTED ALMONDS**

DRESSING

3 TBSP	**PARMESAN CHEESE,** GRATED
¼ CUP	**ORANGE JUICE**
1 TBSP	**RED ONION,** CHOPPED
1 TBSP	**VINEGAR**
½ CUP	**EXTRA-VIRGIN OLIVE OIL** OR **CANOLA OIL**
•	**SALT AND PEPPER,** TO TASTE

A heavy dairy meal needs this salad as the perfect compliment.

1   In a large bowl, combine the lettuce, oranges, and scallions.

2   To prepare dressing, in a medium bowl, combine the parmesan cheese, juice, and red onion. Whisk in the vinegar and oil. Season with salt and pepper.

3   Just before serving, add the avocado to the salad bowl. Add toasted almonds. Toss with 6 Tablespoons dressing or to taste. Refrigerate remaining dressing.

SWEETHEART SALAD

1 HEAD	**ROMAINE LETTUCE,** CHOPPED
1 CUP	**PINEAPPLE,** FRESH, CUBED
¼ CUP	**DRIED APRICOTS,** CHOPPED
¼ CUP	**DRIED CRANBERRIES**
¼ CUP	**ROASTED ALMONDS**
1	**GREEN APPLE**

DRESSING

3 TBSP	**LEMON JUICE**
2 TBSP	**OIL**
¼ TSP	**SALT**
1 TBSP	**SUGAR**

A slightly tart dressing complements the sweet ingredients in this salad. It's named after my sweetheart sister-in-law who shared this recipe with me.

1 In a large bowl, combine lettuce, pineapple, apricots, cranberries, and almonds.

2 Combine dressing ingredients.

3 Right before serving, core and slice the apple, with peel on, add to salad, and toss with dressing.

6-4-2 SALAD

1 HEAD	**ROMAINE LETTUCE,** TORN INTO BITE-SIZE PIECES
½ CUP	**POMEGRANATE SEEDS**
1	**SMALL RED ONION,** THINLY SLICED
6 SLICES	**PASTRAMI,** THINLY SLICED

DRESSING

6 TBSP	**VINEGAR**
4 TBSP	**OIL**
2 TBSP	**SUGAR**
•	**SALT AND PEPPER,** TO TASTE

This is my mother-in-law's Friday-night staple. It's impossible to forget the dressing recipe, since it's just remembering the proportions; you can make it in any amount. All you need is a spoon to whisk it together.

You can easily substitute smoked turkey or any other deli meat that you prefer.

1   Add salad ingredients to a large serving bowl.

2   Whisk dressing ingredients together. Toss with salad just before serving.

ORZO & DILL SALAD

YIELD 6-8 SERVINGS

1½ CUP	**CARROTS,** DICED
4 CLOVES	**GARLIC,** PEELED AND CRUSHED
2 TBSP	**OIL**
1 LB	**ORZO,** COOKED ACCORDING TO PACKAGE DIRECTIONS AND DRAINED
2 TBSP	**LEMON JUICE**
¼ CUP	**OLIVE OIL**
4	**SCALLIONS,** WHITE AND LIGHT GREEN PARTS ONLY, COARSELY CHOPPED
¼ CUP	**FRESH CHOPPED DILL**
½ TBSP	**SALT**
•	**BLACK PEPPER,** TO TASTE

1   Preheat oven to 350°F.

2   Toss carrots and garlic with oil on a baking sheet. Roast in oven for 20 minutes. Let cool.

3   Toss roasted carrots with orzo, lemon juice, olive oil, scallions, dill, salt, and pepper.

4   Serve at room temperature.

AVOCADO PASTA SALAD

YIELD 6-8 SERVINGS

1 LB	**SMALL SHELL PASTA**
4 TBSP	**OLIVE OIL**
1 TSP	**SALT**
½ TSP	**BLACK PEPPER**
1 TBSP	**DRIED PARSLEY FLAKES**
2 CLOVES	**GARLIC,** PEELED AND CRUSHED
1	**RIPE AVOCADO,** CUBED
2 CUPS	**HEARTS OF PALM,** OPTIONAL
1 PINT	**CHERRY TOMATOES,** SLICED IN HALF
½ CUP	**PINE NUTS**

1   Cook pasta according to package directions. Drain.

2   In a large serving bowl, combine warm pasta with olive oil, salt, pepper, parsley flakes, garlic, avocado, and hearts of palm, if desired. Store in airtight container until ready to serve.

3   When ready to serve, toss with tomatoes and pine nuts.

GEMELLI BASIL PASTA SALAD

PARVE

Gemelli means "twins" in Italian. These medium-sized pasta shapes resemble two short pieces of tubular spaghetti twisted together. Use gemelli in entrées, side dishes, oven bakes, and cold salads.

1   Prepare pasta according to package directions. Drain and set aside.

2   Preheat oven to 475°F.

3   Place pepper strips onto a baking sheet lined with parchment paper. Spray with nonstick cooking spray. Season with salt and pepper. Roast for 20 minutes.

4   Meanwhile, combine all ingredients for dressing. Toss with pasta and peppers.

5   Leftovers can be refrigerated for up to 5 days.

YIELD 6-8 SERVINGS

1 LB	**GEMELLI PASTA**
2	**RED PEPPERS,** SLICED INTO THIN STRIPS
2	**YELLOW PEPPERS,** SLICED INTO THIN STRIPS
•	**NONSTICK COOKING SPRAY**
•	**SALT AND PEPPER**

DRESSING

⅓ CUP	**KETCHUP**
⅔ CUP	**MAYONNAISE**
2 CLOVES	**GARLIC,** PEELED AND CRUSHED
2 TBSP	**OIL**
¼ CUP	**VINEGAR**
1 TBSP	**BROWN SUGAR**
2 TBSP	**DRIED BASIL**
1 TSP	**SALT**
1 TSP	**BALSAMIC VINEGAR**
•	**BLACK PEPPER**

DUO SALAD WITH POPPY DRESSING

YIELD 6-8 SERVINGS

4-5 SLICES	**PASTRAMI**
½ LB	**BONELESS CHICKEN BREAST**
1 HEAD	**ROMAINE LETTUCE,** CUT INTO BITE-SIZED PIECES
3 CUPS	**SPINACH LEAVES**
1	**MEDIUM RED ONION,** SLICED INTO HALF-MOONS
½ CUP	**HONEY GLAZED ALMONDS,** COARSELY CHOPPED

This is the ultimate chicken salad. A neighbor of mine once said, "Some salads are ignored by all the men on the table and some salads are just perfect and the men can't get enough." This one was made for men (and the woman who don't mind a really good salad).

If you don't use or can't find spinach, simply replace it with additional romaine lettuce.

1 Preheat oven to 475°F.

2 Spread the pastrami slices on a baking sheet. Bake for 10 minutes or until pastrami is toasted. Let cool and cut into strips.

3 Combine all marinade ingredients (see facing page) in a ziptop bag. Lightly pound the chicken and add to bag. Marinate for 20 minutes. Discard marinade and add chicken to a preheated grill pan or skillet. Cook over medium heat, turning after 3-4 minutes or when chicken turns white. When it is cooked through, remove chicken from pan and cut into strips.

4 To prepare dressing (see facing page), combine sugar, onion, vinegar, mustard, and salt. Gradually whisk in the oil. Stir in the poppy seeds.

5 Toss salad ingredients together with the desired amount of dressing. There will be dressing left over.

CHICKEN MARINADE

1 TBSP	LEMON JUICE
1 TBSP	OLIVE OIL
1 CLOVE	GARLIC, PEELED AND CRUSHED
½ TSP	SALT
⅛ TSP	PEPPER
½ TSP	OREGANO

POPPY DRESSING

½ CUP	SUGAR
2-3 TBSP	ONION, CHOPPED
⅓ CUP	VINEGAR
1 TSP	YELLOW MUSTARD
1 TSP	SALT
1 CUP	OIL
2 TSP	POPPY SEEDS

CHICKEN FAJITAS SALAD

YIELD 1-2 MAIN DISH
SERVINGS OR 5 SIDE
DISH SERVINGS

1 HEAD	**ROMAINE LETTUCE**
½ CUP	**CHERRY TOMATOES,** HALVED
½ CUP	**CROUTONS,** OPTIONAL
¼ LB	**PREPARED CHICKEN FAJITAS** (RECIPE P. 192)

DRESSING

4 TBSP	**MAYONNAISE**
1 TBSP	**LEMON JUICE**
1 CLOVE	**GARLIC,** PEELED AND CRUSHED
1 TSP	**SUGAR**
1 TSP	**MUSTARD**
½ TSP	**SALT**
⅛ TSP	**BLACK PEPPER**
5 TBSP	**OIL**

While some consider salad a side dish, I enjoy chicken salads as a main dish, whether at lunch or dinner. Round out the evening meal with a soup or baked potato on the side. You can add any of your favorite vegetables and make use of the chicken you might have left from last night's dinner. (See recipe on page 192)

1 Gently toss together lettuce, tomatoes, croutons, and chicken.

2 To prepare dressing, place all ingredients, except oil, into a bowl. Use an immersion blender to combine while slowly drizzling in the oil.

3 Add dressing to the salad just before serving, about 2-3 Tablespoons for each head of lettuce. Any remaining dressing will keep well in the refrigerator for a few days.

WARM SWEET POTATO SALAD

2½ LBS	**SWEET POTATOES** (PREFERABLY 5 SMALLER ONES)
DASH	**SALT**

DRESSING

3 TBSP	**LIGHT OLIVE OIL** OR **CANOLA OIL**
1 TBSP	**CREAMY DIJON MUSTARD**
½ TBSP	**DRIED CILANTRO**
½ TSP	**SALT**
¼ TSP	**BLACK PEPPER**
1 CLOVE	**GARLIC,** PEELED AND CRUSHED

Sweet potatoes are so good on their own, it's a shame to add marshmallows, brown sugar, or any other sweet ingredient that turns them into a sugary side dish. I like them this way so I can taste their natural sweetness.

This salad is best served at room temperature.

1 Wash the potatoes well and trim the ends. Place the potatoes into a 6-quart pot and cover them with cold water. Add a dash of salt to the pot and bring the water to a boil.

2 Lower the heat and cook for 1 hour or until potatoes are soft when you pierce them with a fork. Drain off the water. Let the potatoes cool slightly, then peel and cube them.

3 Combine dressing ingredients. Toss the cubed potatoes with the dressing. Serve warm or at room temperature.

SALATIM AND A CHAVITAH

There's a standing joke in my friend's family. If one can't find what to eat from an entire selection of food, they say, "Oh, you want salatim and a chavita."

The story originated a couple of years ago when a young Israeli man was a guest in their home. In typical American Hungarian fashion, the dairy meal was lavish and full of dairy delicacies including cheese blintzes, fish, creamy potatoes, a choice of pastas and a large selection of cheesecakes and cheese buns for dessert. Yet, the young man had not taken anything on his plate. When the host asked him if anything was wrong with the food, he said no. Yet, he still hadn't eaten a thing.

Finally the host asked, "Is there something specifically that you like, that I can offer you?

"Well," he replied, "Salatim and a chavitah. Dips and an omelette.

DIPS & SAUCES

TECHINA

PARVE

YIELD 5 CUPS

1 17.64oz CONTAINER	**TAHINI** (SESAME PASTE)
•	**WATER**
¼ CUP	**FRESH LEMON JUICE**
½ TBSP	**SALT**
4-5 CLOVES	**GARLIC,** PEELED AND CRUSHED
1 DASH	**CHILI POWDER**

Even the simplest falafel sandwich must include techina. This is a basic recipe you can adjust to your liking.

1 Empty the container of tahini into a bowl. Fill the empty container with water and add water to the tahini. Stir to combine.

2 Add lemon juice, salt, garlic, and chili powder. Mix well by hand or in a blender.

CHUNKY HUMMUS

PARVE

YIELD 2 CUPS

1 14oz CAN	**GARBANZO BEANS** (CHICKPEAS)
1 HANDFUL	**PARSLEY LEAVES,** OPTIONAL
1 CLOVE	**GARLIC,** PEELED
½ TSP	**SALT**
¼ TSP	**GROUND CUMIN**
3 TBSP	**FRESH LEMON JUICE**
4 TBSP	**WATER**
4 TBSP	**TAHINI**
2 TBSP	**OLIVE OIL** + ADDITIONAL FOR GARNISH

You can make the hummus thicker by adding less water or make it creamier by blending the chickpeas for a few seconds longer before adding the liquid ingredients.

1 Drain and rinse the garbanzo beans. Reserve a few chickpeas to use as garnish.

2 Place remaining chickpeas into a food processor with the parsley (if using), garlic, salt, and cumin. Blend until chunky. Add lemon juice, water, tahini, and olive oil; blend for a few seconds longer.

3 Garnish with additional olive oil and reserved chickpeas.

NOTE

When purchasing tahini paste, choose an Israeli brand — they make it best.

Tahini is defined as a paste made of ground sesame seeds, and is used as an ingredient to make tahina, or techina, the term we use to describe the delicious dressing we pour onto falafel. However, there is really only a difference of pronunciation between the two, as either can mean "a paste made of ground sesame seeds."

SPICY OLIVES

YIELD 2 CUPS

2½	**SERRANO PEPPERS,** STEMS REMOVED
2 CUPS	**SMALL SPANISH PITTED OLIVES,** DRAINED
½ CUP	**EXTRA-LIGHT OLIVE OIL**
1 HEAD	**GARLIC,** PEELED AND MINCED

Why eat plain olives when you can have them spiced?

- Thinly slice peppers, retaining seeds. Combine all ingredients in a bowl or container.

TARTAR SAUCE

YIELD ¾ CUP

8 TBSP	**MAYONNAISE**
4 CLOVES	**GARLIC,** PEELED AND MINCED
2	**SMALL ISRAELI PICKLES,** DICED
3	**SCALLIONS,** DICED (WHITE PART ONLY)
HANDFUL	**PARSLEY,** CHOPPED
2 TBSP	**LEMON JUICE**
•	**SALT AND PEPPER,** TO TASTE

This is the perfect accompaniment to fried fish. If you are in a rush, you can blend the ingredients instead of dicing.

- In a small bowl, combine all ingredients. Adjust seasoning to taste.

JALAPEÑO DIP

This is spicy. You have been warned! If you can handle some heat, this will become your staple at every meal. Make sure you wear gloves when deseeding the pepper, and avoid touching your eyes afterward.

1	LONG HOT PEPPER
2	JALAPEÑO PEPPERS
3	SERRANO PEPPERS
1½ CUPS	MAYONNAISE
2-3 CLOVES	GARLIC, TO TASTE

1 Remove the stems of the peppers, leaving the seeds intact.

2 Using a blender or food processor, combine all ingredients until smooth.

PIZZA DIPPING SAUCE

American pizza is always served with a side of fries, while Israeli pizza is always served with the pizza joint's secret dipping sauce. It's quite addictive, and once you start dipping, you won't be able to eat plain pizza anymore.

½ CUP	MAYONNAISE
½ CUP	TOMATO SAUCE
¼ TSP	ITALIAN SEASONING
¼-½ TSP	CAYENNE OR GROUND RED PEPPER, TO TASTE
¼ TSP	GARLIC POWDER
PINCH	SALT
2 TBSP	WATER, OPTIONAL, AS NEEDED

• Stir ingredients together until well combined.

TOMATO DIP

The ratio of tomato to garlic in this dip really depends on your taste. Some use only one clove per tomato — I like to use a bit more. You can add more to your liking. Peel the tomatoes for a smoother dip, if you prefer.

YIELD 2½ CUPS

3	**LARGE TOMATOES,** QUARTERED
3 CLOVES	**GARLIC,** PEELED
½ CUP	**OIL**
1 TSP	**SALT** + MORE, TO TASTE
¼–½ TSP	**BLACK PEPPER**

1 Blend the tomatoes and garlic for 2 minutes.

2 Adjust seasoning to taste.

SPICY HONEY-MUSTARD SAUCE

This is part of my grandmother's Shabbos morning spread, though I can never make it taste as good as she can.

Delicious with lox and smoked fish.

YIELD 3 CUPS

2 CUPS	**MAYONNAISE**
2 TBSP	**YELLOW MUSTARD**
1 CUP	**HONEY**
1 TBSP	**COARSLY GROUND BLACK PEPPER**

1 In a bowl or container, whisk together mayonnaise, mustard, and honey until well combined.

2 Stir in black pepper.

SLICED GARLIC DIP

For lovers of garlic, spreading this dip on a warm piece of challah would definitely be considered *oneg Shabbos*, one of the pleasures of Shabbos. Adjust the pepper to your liking.

YIELD 1 CUP

1 CUP	**OIL**
3 HEADS	**GARLIC** (ABOUT 36 CLOVES), PEELED AND THINLY SLICED
1 TSP	**SALT**
⅓ TSP	**SWEET PAPRIKA**
½ - 1 TSP	**CRUSHED RED PEPPER,** TO TASTE

1 Heat oil in a skillet over medium-high heat. Add the garlic; fry 10-15 minutes or until golden brown, stirring occasionally.

2 Remove from heat and add salt, paprika, and red pepper.

3 Place into an airtight container. Serve at room temperature.

CHAYA'S CHATZILIM SALAD

PHOTO PAGE 77
PARVE

This is eggplant like you've never had it before. My friend Chaya doesn't write down any of her recipes. She makes this eggplant salad every week, but couldn't tell me the recipe. So, the next time she prepared it, I went to her house and stood next to her. I measured each ingredient into a cup, handed it to her, and she poured. When she was done, I measured what was left and figured out how much she had used. The results were delicious, and I've continued to make this many times — now that I know the recipe!

1. Wash eggplants well and slice into thin rounds, about ¼ inch thick.

2. Place eggplant slices into a large bowl and salt well. Let them "sweat" a minimum of 20 minutes to overnight. This removes most of the bitter juices. Wash well and pat dry.

3. In a skillet over medium heat, heat a liberal amount of oil for frying. Fry eggplant slices for 6-9 minutes on each side until brown/black, crunchy, and thin, like chips. Mix well with remaining ingredients. The eggplant will break apart as you stir. Refrigerate. Serve cold or at room temperature.

YIELD 3 CUPS

2	**LARGE EGGPLANTS**
•	**SALT**
•	**OIL,** FOR FRYING
⅔ CUP	MINUS 1 TBSP **VINEGAR**
⅓ CUP	**WATER**
⅔ CUP	MINUS 1 TBSP **SUGAR**
4 CLOVES	**GARLIC,** PEELED AND MINCED

THAI SWEET CHILI SAUCE

2 CLOVES	**GARLIC,** PEELED
½ CUP	**SUGAR**
¾ CUP	**WATER**
¼ CUP	**VINEGAR**
½ TSP	**SALT**
½ LARGE	**RED BELL PEPPER,** SEEDS AND STEMS DISCARDED
1½-2 TSP	**RED PEPPER FLAKES**
1 TBSP	**CORNSTARCH**
2 TBSP	**WATER**
2 TBSP	**HONEY,** OPTIONAL

Thai Sweet Chili Sauce is one of the greatest condiments that exists. While I buy a ready-made version all the time, it's really easy and quick to make it yourself.

Sweet Chili is a sweet and spicy dipping sauce. Most recipes call for red jalapeño or chili peppers. Since the red ones aren't available all year round where I live, I substitute a red bell pepper with some crushed red pepper flakes. I use the sweet chili as a dipping sauce for eggrolls and wontons, in stir fries, and, surprisingly, it tastes amazing with pizza!

1 Using a food processor, blend together garlic, sugar, ¼ cup water, vinegar, salt, bell pepper, and red pepper flakes until well combined.

2 Transfer to a 2-quart pot and bring to a boil. Lower heat and simmer for 5 minutes.

3 Dissolve cornstarch in 2 Tablespoons water and add to mixture. Stir well until sauce thickens slightly.

4 Add 2 Tablespoons honey, if desired.

5 Taste and adjust seasonings.

GARLIC MAYONNAISE

YIELD 5½ CUPS

3 CLOVES	**GARLIC,** PEELED
•	**JUICE OF 1½ LEMONS**
2	**EGGS**
½ TSP	**SALT**
DASH	**BLACK PEPPER**
4 CUPS	**OIL**

Technically speaking this recipe is an aioli. Aioli is a garlic-flavored mayonnaise. Many have a *minhag* not to use garlic on Pesach, but you can easily substitute half a medium onion. Chock full of flavor, this is not another boring mayonnaise. Be sure to use fresh eggs that were refrigerated and it will last 5-6 days in the refrigerator.

- In a blender or food processor, combine the garlic, lemon juice, eggs, salt, and pepper. With the motor running, pour in the oil in a thin stream. Start very gradually and then quicken the pace as you come to the end. Blend until this is thoroughly combined and the mayonnaise is emulsified. Do not overmix. When it is emulsified, it's done.

ADDITIONAL SAUCES

MATCHES MADE IN THE KITCHEN

A recipe doesn't have to be complicated to be delicious. Next time you're experimenting in the kitchen, make sure your dish includes flavors that complement.

Almonds + Chocolate
Apples + Vanilla ice cream
Avocados + Tomatoes
Bananas + Chocolate
Beef + Mushrooms
Blueberries + Lemon
Cauliflower + Breadcrumbs
Chestnuts + Apples
Chocolate + Coffee or Nuts
Corned beef + Mustard
Cucumbers + Dill
Eggplant + Garlic
Grapefruit + Honey
Mango + Raspberries
Mushrooms + Wine
Pears + Brandy
Pecans + Caramel
Pomegranates + Chocolate
Potatoes + Salt
Rhubarb + Strawberry
Romaine + Olive oil
Rice + Nuts
Sea bass + Peppers
Sweet potatoes + Orange
Sweetbreads + Mushrooms
Tongue + Horseradish
Zucchini + Parsley

SIDE DISHES

ONION BLOSSOMS

4 LARGE	**SWEET ONIONS** (OR 6 MEDIUM, OR 8 SMALL)
•	**OIL,** FOR FRYING

BEER BATTER

1¾ CUP	**FLOUR**
1½ TSP	**BAKING POWDER**
1½ TSP	**SALT**
3 TBSP	**YELLOW CORNMEAL**
1½ CUPS (12oz)	**LIGHT BEER**
1	**EGG,** LIGHTLY BEATEN

HONEY-MUSTARD DIPPING SAUCE

3 TBSP	**MAYONNAISE**
3 TBSP	**DIJON MUSTARD**
1½ TBSP	**HONEY**
•	**SALT AND PEPPER,** TO TASTE

Onion Blossoms, Blooming Onion, Unbelievable Onion … this appetizer is one of the most brilliant new additions to fast-food menus. With some simple slicing, the onion opens up to form the shape of a flower. With a small bowl of dipping sauce in the center, it really offers a beautiful presentation without much effort.

1 To prepare the beer batter, combine dry ingredients in a large bowl. Add the beer and egg; stir to combine. Refrigerate for 10-15 minutes.

2 Meanwhile, trim the ends of the onions, being careful that the root end stays intact. To form the blossom, cut each onion into 8-10 wedges. Cuts should not extend all the way to the root so that the onion remains in one piece.

3 Heat the oil in a pot or deep fryer over medium-high heat. Dip the onions into the beer batter, making sure to separate the wedges so that the batter covers all layers. Fry the blossoms in the hot oil for 8 minutes, turning if necessary. Drain on paper towels.

4 To prepare honey-mustard sauce, combine ingredients in a bowl and mix well.

5 Serve blossoms with dipping sauce.

CARAMELIZED SHALLOTS

YIELD 5-6 SERVINGS

15	**SHALLOTS,** PEELED, ROOT END INTACT
2 TBSP	**OIL**
1 TBSP	**SUGAR**
•	**SALT AND PEPPER,** TO TASTE
•	**WATER,** AS NEEDED

So many recipes use shallots as an alternative to onions. I think it's a waste of a delicious shallot to dice it and allow it to get lost in a complicated dish. Shallots are so delicious on their own that I can't bring myself to drown their flavor with other ingredients.

1 Heat the oil in a medium pot over medium heat. Add the shallots, sugar, salt, and pepper. Cook for 2-3 minutes, stirring occasionally.

2 Add just enough water to cover the shallots. Raise heat to medium-high and cook until the water evaporates, stirring occasionally.

3 When the water has fully evaporated, cook for an additional 2-3 minutes, watching carefully to prevent burning. Remove from heat when the shallots turn golden brown.

ORANGE-GLAZED ROOT VEGETABLES

YIELD 4-6 SERVINGS

2	PARSNIPS
2	SWEET POTATOES
1	LARGE TURNIP
2	CARROTS
1	MEDIUM CELERY KNOB
3 TBSP	ORANGE JUICE
2 TBSP	OLIVE OIL
1 TBSP	SUGAR
1 TSP	SALT
PINCH	BLACK PEPPER

If you're trying to watch your waist, this side dish may help a bit. I'm not big into tricking my kids and I prefer telling them what they are eating, but when I made this, my children assumed it was potatoes and sweet potatoes. They ate peacefully and filled up. Only the one with finer taste buds realized something was different.

1 Preheat oven to 475°F. Line a baking sheet with foil or parchment paper.

2 Peel all vegetables and cut into evenly sized chunks (about 1-inch). In a large bowl, toss vegetables with the juice, oil, sugar, salt, and pepper.

3 Spread vegetables on baking sheet. Bake for 1 hour or until vegetables are tender.

SQUASH SOUFFLÉS

YIELD 8 SERVINGS

- •   **WATER AS NEEDED**
- 5   **LARGE ZUCCHINI SQUASH**
  (OR 8 SMALL)
- 3   **EGGS**
- ½ CUP   **MAYONNAISE**
- 2 TBSP   **FLOUR**
- 1 TSP   **SALT**
- ⅛ TSP   **BLACK PEPPER**
- ¼ TSP   **BAKING POWDER,**
  OPTIONAL

R. Englard makes this soufflé all year round. On Pesach, she simply substitutes potato starch for the flour.

1   Preheat oven to 350°F.

2   Bring a pot of water to a boil. Wash squash well, add to pot, and boil whole for 15 minutes. Remove squash from the pot. Allow to cool; peel and grate. Strain the grated squash very well, pressing out all the excess liquid. Place drained squash into a large bowl.

3   Add eggs, mayonnaise, flour, salt, black pepper, and baking powder, if using. Using a fork, mix until well combined.

4   Divide between individual ramekins or pour into one deep 10-inch round pan. Bake for 45 minutes to 1 hour, until lightly browned.

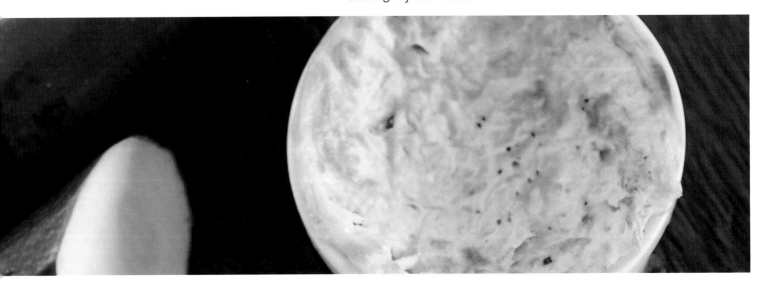

SUNFLOWER GREEN BEANS

PARVE

1 Preheat oven to 450°F.

2 Place green beans and red pepper into a bowl. Add oil, honey, salt, and pepper. Toss to coat.

3 Spread over baking sheet lined with parchment paper.

4 Roast green bean mixture in oven for 15 minutes. Add sunflower seeds and bake for an additional 2-3 minutes.

YIELD 4-6 SERVINGS

1½ LB	**FRESH GREEN BEANS,** ENDS TRIMMED
1	**RED BELL PEPPER,** SLICED INTO STRIPS
2 TBSP	**OIL**
1 TBSP	**HONEY**
½ TSP	**SALT**
•	**BLACK PEPPER,** TO TASTE
¼ CUP	**SALTED SUNFLOWER SEEDS**

BUTTERNUT SQUASH WITH GRAPES & SHALLOTS

YIELD 4-6 SERVINGS

1-2 LARGE	**BUTTERNUT SQUASH**
1 CUP	**RED GRAPES**
5-6	**SHALLOTS,** PEELED
3 TBSP	**HONEY**
4 TBSP	**OIL**
1 TSP	**SALT**
¼ TSP	**BLACK PEPPER**

When choosing a butternut squash, pick one that has a larger top, with a more even shape, so that the slices come out the same size. To save time, you can ask the manager at your local fruit store or supermarket to cut the squash into slices.

1 Preheat oven to 450°F.

2 Peel the squash. Cut off the bottom and use a spoon to scoop out the seeds. Slice each squash crosswise into 10-12 rounds, each about ½ inch thick. Three slices will have a hole, but the rest should be nice and pretty.

3 Spread the butternut squash, grapes, and shallots on a baking sheet lined with parchment paper.

4 In a small bowl, combine the honey, oil, salt, and black pepper. Drizzle or smear it onto the vegetables and fruit. Bake for 1 hour.

DIJON RED POTATO WEDGES

PARVE

YIELD 4-6 SERVINGS

6 TBSP	**DIJON MUSTARD**
3 TBSP	**OIL**
2 CLOVES	**GARLIC,** PEELED AND CRUSHED
1 TBSP	**LEMON JUICE**
1 TSP	**PARSLEY FLAKES**
½ TSP	**SALT**
¼ TSP	**BLACK PEPPER**
2 LB	**SMALL RED POTATOES,** WITH SKIN, CUT INTO WEDGES

A few days before a family get-together, my menu was almost complete. I needed one more side dish. I called my sister.

"I have rice, zucchini, and sweet potatoes," I told her. "What else should I make?"

"Potatoes," she quickly replied.

"But I'm making sweet potatoes," I responded.

I heard a sigh through the phone, and then she ended the argument with a profound statement. "That's orange, so it counts as a vegetable."

So I made potatoes.

1 Preheat oven to 425°F

2 In a large bowl, combine the mustard, oil, garlic, lemon juice, parsley, salt, and pepper. Add the potatoes and stir to coat.

3 Spread the potatoes over a baking sheet lined with parchment paper. Roast for 45 minutes, turning over halfway through baking time.

BREAKFAST HOME FRIES

PARVE

YIELD 2-4 SERVINGS

3	**LARGE POTATOES** WITH SKINS
4 TBSP	**OIL** + ADDITIONAL TBSP IF NEEDED
¾ TSP	**SALT,** DIVIDED
PINCH	**BLACK PEPPER**
1	**LARGE ONION,** CUT INTO CHUNKS

The history of French fries is not that simple. Though the French claim it as their own, legend holds that Thomas Jefferson, Founding Father and the third president of the United States, introduced French fries to American shores. He is also credited with naming them "French fries" in the late 1700s, describing the dish as "potatoes, fried in a French manner." "French" refers to the method of cutting the potatoes, as "to french" means to cut into thin strips. Belgians, however, claim that fries have been a national snack since 1680, served in a paper cone with a creamy mayonnaise dipping sauce.

1 Wash the potatoes and cut into ¾-inch chunks.

2 Heat oil in a large nonstick skillet over high heat. Add the potatoes, half the salt, and the pepper. Cover and cook 5 minutes.

3 Uncover, add the onion and 1 additional Tablespoon of oil, if necessary. Lower heat to medium, cover, and cook an additional 5 minutes.

4 Uncover and cook for an additional 15 minutes, stirring frequently. Toss with remaining salt before serving.

NOTE

Traditional fries are double fried. During the first frying, the oil is heated to 325°F and the potatoes are cooked until soft but not brown. The fries are then drained on paper towels or in brown paper bags. Then the temperature of the oil is raised to 375°F and the fries are returned to fry for 4 minutes or until golden and crispy. The first frying can be done ahead of time, and the second right before serving.

After cutting the potatoes, place the strips into ice-cold water for a few minutes. This washes out the starch, making the fries less sticky after the first frying and crispier after the second.

You don't need to pull out your deep fryer to enjoy French fries. Home fries, a breakfast staple, are just as delicious and made in a skillet.

SPICY FRIES

YIELD 4 SERVINGS

2-3 LBS	**POTATOES** OR **FROZEN FRENCH FRIES**
•	**OIL,** FOR FRYING

BATTER

1 CUP	**FLOUR**
1 TSP	**GARLIC POWDER**
1 TSP	**ONION POWDER**
1½ TSP	**SALT**
1 TSP	**PAPRIKA**
¾ CUP	**WATER**
•	**CAYENNE** OR **CAJUN SEASONING,** TO TASTE, OPTIONAL

I usually use frozen fries when I make these, since it's quicker and the texture is just like the Cajun fries I'd order at my local pizza shop. If you like them spicy, add cayenne or Cajun seasoning to the batter.

1   If using fresh potatoes, peel potatoes and slice into thin strips. Preheat the oil in a deep skillet or large pot over high heat.

2   For the batter, combine flour and seasonings, adding water gradually to form a batter. Add more water if necessary until the batter can be drizzled from a spoon.

3   Dip the potatoes into the batter one at a time and slip into the hot oil. Fry until golden brown and crispy. Remove and drain on paper towels.

NOTE

Make sure the oil is very hot (375°F). To test, place one French fry in the oil. It should sizzle and pop right up. If it sits too long on the bottom, the oil is not hot enough. The hotter the oil, the less greasy the fries will be.

SWEET POTATO & PASTRAMI POCKETS

YIELD 16 POCKETS

1	**ONION**, DICED
3 TBSP	**OIL**
2 CUPS	**SWEET POTATO**, DICED INTO ½-INCH CUBES (ABOUT 1 LARGE)
½ TSP	**SALT**
¼ TSP	**BLACK PEPPER**
1 CUP	**PASTRAMI**, CUT INTO ½ INCH CUBES (A LITTLE LESS THAN ½ LB)
2 TBSP	**APRICOT JAM**
1½ TBSP	**SOY SAUCE**
½ TSP	**DRIED PARSLEY FLAKES**
4	**MALAWAH DOUGH ROUNDS**
1	**EGG, BEATEN FOR EGG WASH**, OPTIONAL

Malawah or Malawach dough is a great choice for a dough to fill with your favorite appetizer. Originally a staple of Yemenite Jews, it consists of thin layers of puff pastry brushed with oil. You can find in the freezer section of any local supermarket. Since the dough is brushed with oil, the end result is much crispier than puff pastry. I imagine if you pan fry it, it would be extra amazing, but due to the calorie count, I decided against it. Malawah dough comes in 8-inch disks in a package containing 6-7 rounds. It takes literally 5-8 mintues to defrost, so don't defrost too early. Once the dough has completely defrosted, it's very difficult to work with.

1 Preheat oven to 375°F.

2 In a skillet, sauté the onion in the oil for 5 minutes. Add the sweet potatoes, salt, and pepper. Cook for 5-6 minutes. Cover and continue cooking for 5 minutes (don't open the pan). Mix and test one cube to make sure they are slightly soft.

3 Add the pastrami cubes, apricot jam, soy sauce, and parsley flakes.

4 Sauté to 1-2 minutes, stirring until all ingredients are well incorporated.

5 Defrost the dough for 5-8 minutes. Using a rolling pin, roll out one sheet at a time into a 10-inch circle. Using a 4-inch round cookie cutter, cut out 4 circles. ▶

NOTE

TERIYAKI DIPPING SAUCE

Here is a quick dipping sauce to go with the pockets.

½ CUP	**SOY SAUCE**
½ CUP	**SUGAR**
1 CLOVE	**GARLIC,** PEELED AND CRUSHED
1 TSP	**WHISKEY**

Place soy sauce, sugar, and garlic into a small pot. Cook over medium heat for 5-7 minutes. Remove from heat and stir in whiskey.

6 Place 1 Tablespoon filling into the center of each circle. Fold dough in half and pinch ends close. Place on a baking sheet lined with parchment paper. Alternatively, you can cut the dough into 4 parts and fold each triangle in half.

7 Brush with beaten egg. Bake for 20 minutes or until bottoms are just golden.

8 When re-warming in the oven, keep uncovered to prevent the pockets from becoming soggy.

SWEET-POTATO FRIES

Using the oven and the silicone baking mat achieves a fried taste without excess oil or mess. If you don't have a silicone mat, simply line the baking sheet with parchment paper and bake for 40 minutes to an hour before tossing with the seasonings.

YIELD 4 SERVINGS

2-3	**SWEET POTATOES,** PEELED AND CUT INTO FRENCH-FRY STRIPS
3 TBSP	**OIL**
½ TSP	**SUGAR**
½ TSP	**SALT**
½ TSP	**PARSLEY FLAKES**

1 On a heavy-duty aluminum baking sheet lined with a silicone baking mat, toss potatoes with oil and spread in one layer.

2 Bake at 450°F for ½ hour until lightly browned and crispy at the edges.

3 Combine sugar, salt, and parsley flakes; toss potatoes in the mixture.

GARLIC FRIES

These fries deserve a dip like a light Caesar dressing. In a pinch, a good mayonnaise works well. For less kick, reduce the black pepper and chili powder.

YIELD 4 SERVINGS

3 LB	**YUKON GOLD POTATOES,** WITH PEEL, CUT INTO WEDGES
•	**HOT WATER,** TO COVER
⅓ CUP	**OLIVE OIL**
8 CLOVES	**GARLIC,** PEELED AND CRUSHED
6 TBSP	**CORNSTARCH**
¾ TBSP	**SALT**
½ TSP	**BLACK PEPPER,** OR TO TASTE
¼ TSP	**CHILI POWDER,** OR TO TASTE

1 Preheat oven to 425°F.

2 Slice potatoes into evenly sized wedges. Soak potato wedges in very hot water for 10 minutes. Drain and dry well. Combine oil and crushed garlic in a bowl. Toss potato with garlic mixture. Add cornstarch and spices to the bowl and toss well until evenly distributed.

3 Line two baking sheets with parchment paper. Spread the potato wedges on the sheets. Bake for 40 minutes.

AVOCADO WONTONS

YIELD 20-24 WONTONS

2	**RIPE AVOCADOS**
2 TBSP	**LEMON JUICE**
2	**SCALLIONS,** WHITE AND LIGHT GREEN PARTS ONLY, CHOPPED
1 TBSP	**FRESH PARSLEY,** CHOPPED
•	**SALT AND BLACK PEPPER,** TO TASTE
20-24	**ROUND WONTON WRAPPERS**
•	**OIL FOR FRYING**

To prevent wonton wrappers from drying out, always keep them covered with a damp cloth until ready to be filled.

1 Dice avocado into small pieces. Combine with lemon juice, scallions, parsley, salt, and pepper. Place a scant teaspoon of filling into the center of a wonton round. Dip your finger into water and wet the edges of the wonton. Press edges together, forming a half circle, and seal. Continue with remaining wontons.

2 Heat oil in a small pot or deep fryer. Add wontons, a few at a time. Do not crowd wontons in the pot.

3 Deep fry for roughly 2 minutes, until lightly browned. Remove from oil and drain on paper towels.

4 Serve immediately.

MEXICAN RICE

YIELD 4 SERVINGS

1 LARGE CLOVE	**GARLIC,** PEELED
¼	**MEDIUM ONION**
4	**PLUM TOMATOES,** CUT INTO CHUNKS
¾ CUP	**WATER**
4 TBSP	**OIL**
1 CUP	**RICE,** UNCOOKED
1 TSP	**CHICKEN-FLAVORED CONSOMMÉ POWDER**
1 TSP	**SALT**

I can't vouch that this is a truly authentic Mexican recipe (although I did learn how to make it from a Mexican woman I once knew), but I can vouch that it's one of the best tasting rice dishes I make.

1 In a food processor, blend the garlic, onion, tomatoes, and water for a full 5 minutes.

2 Heat the oil in a 2-quart saucepan over high heat. Add the rice and cook, stirring constantly, for 5 minutes.

3 Drain off most of the oil. Add the tomato mixture to the pot and stir. Add the consommé powder and salt.

4 Cook for 5-6 minutes over high heat. Lower the heat, cover, and simmer for 20 minutes.

5 Remove from heat and let the rice rest for a few minutes before serving.

RICE VERMICELLI WITH ROASTED VEGGIES

YIELD 6 SERVINGS

ROASTED VEGETABLES

3 TBSP	**OIL**
¼ TSP	**SALT**
¼ TSP	**SUGAR**
¼ TSP	**PAPRIKA**
¼ TSP	**ONION POWDER**
1 LB	**FROZEN BROCCOLI AND CAULIFLOWER MIX**

RICE VERMICELLI

2 TBSP	**OIL**
1 CUP	**RICE**
¾ CUP	**VERMICELLI PASTA,** UNCOOKED, BROKEN INTO 2-INCH STICKS
2¾ CUPS	**CHICKEN STOCK**
½-1 TSP	**SALT,** TO TASTE
DASH	**BLACK PEPPER**

1 Preheat oven to 350°F.

2 Combine 3 Tablespoons oil with the spices.

3 Place the frozen broccoli and cauliflower into a 9x13-inch pan. Drizzle with spiced oil. Bake, uncovered, for 30 minutes.

4 Wash and drain the rice.

5 In a 2-quart pot, heat 2 Tablespoons oil. Add the rice and vermicelli. Sauté for 2 minutes, stirring occasionally. Add the chicken stock, salt, and pepper. Cover and cook over medium heat for 20 minutes. Turn off the stove. Place a paper towel under the lid and let rest for 5 minutes.

6 Toss with roasted vegetables.

HONEY-MUSTARD COUSCOUS

YIELD 4-6 SERVINGS

2 CLOVES	**GARLIC,** PEELED AND CRUSHED
1 TBSP	**YELLOW MUSTARD**
1 TBSP	**HONEY**
2 TBSP	**VINEGAR**
½ TBSP	**SALT**
¼ CUP	**OIL**
1 LB	**ACINI DI PEPE,** COOKED ACCORDING TO PACKAGE DIRECTIONS
½ CUP	**DRIED CRANBERRIES**
½ CUP	**HONEY-GLAZED PECANS,** CHOPPED

When my brother and sister-in-law were newly married, my sister-in-law mentioned that she was making couscous for dinner. I emphatically replied, "My brother does not like couscous."

I didn't know she was talking about this kind of couscous. Some call this Israeli couscous and others by the Italian name, acini di pepe. In Israel it's called *p'titim*. Unlike its fluffy and grainy cousin, this dish is made up of little balls of toasted pasta. So even if you don't like traditional couscous, if you love orzo-shaped pasta, this is the couscous for you.

1 In a small bowl, combine garlic, mustard, honey, vinegar, salt, and oil. Toss the cooked pasta with the honey-mustard dressing.

2 Add the dried cranberries and honey-glazed pecans just before serving.

COUSCOUS WITH VEGETABLES

I'm not a fan of traditional couscous — but I've grown to love the Israeli version. A pasta rather than a grain, and tasty hot or cold, it's another great base for a delicious pasta salad.

YIELD 4-6 SERVINGS

1	**RED BELL PEPPER,** DICED
1	**YELLOW PEPPER,** DICED
1	**SMALL EGGPLANT,** DICED
2 TBSP	**OIL**
2	**SMALL ZUCCHINI,** CUT INTO HALF MOONS
(8.8OZ) BAG	**ISRAELI COUSCOUS,** COOKED ACCORDING TO PACKAGE DIRECTIONS
3	**SCALLIONS,** WHITE AND LIGHT GREEN PARTS ONLY, SLICED
•	**SALT AND BLACK PEPPER,** TO TASTE

BROWN SUGAR DRESSING

3 TBSP	**VINEGAR**
¼ CUP	**OIL**
1 TBSP	**BROWN SUGAR**
½ TSP	**SALT**
1 CLOVE	**GARLIC,** PEELED AND CRUSHED
⅛ TSP	**BLACK PEPPER**
½ TSP	**SOY SAUCE**

1 Preheat oven to 450°F.

2 Line two baking sheets with parchment paper. Toss the diced peppers and eggplant with oil and spread out on one sheet. Spread the zucchini on the second baking sheet and coat with nonstick spray. Roast for 45 minutes, tossing halfway through.

3 To prepare dressing, combine all ingredients.

4 Toss the prepared couscous with the dressing, vegetables, and the sliced scallions. Add salt and pepper to taste.

5 Serve at room temperature.

CONFETTI ORZO

PARVE

The orzo is delicious on its own, though the red onion cups are an easy way to make this dish extraordinary for special occasions.

YIELD 4 SERVINGS

2 TBSP	**OIL**
1	**MEDIUM ONION,** DICED
5oz	**MUSHROOM,** CLEANED AND SLICED
1	**LARGE TOMATO,** DICED
½ LB	**FROZEN SPINACH,** THAWED AND DRAINED
1 CLOVE	**GARLIC,** PEELED AND CRUSHED
3 TBSP	**SOY SAUCE**
1 LB	**ORZO,** COOKED AND DRAINED
•	**SALT AND PEPPER,** TO TASTE

1 Heat the oil in a large sauté pan over medium heat. Add the onion and cook for 5-6 minutes, until translucent. Add the mushrooms and tomatoes. Cook for 5 minutes. Add spinach and garlic and cook for an additional 5 minutes.

2 Add the soy sauce to the pan and stir. Season with salt and pepper. Add the pasta to the pan and stir to combine. Taste and adjust seasoning.

RED ONION CUPS

PARVE

YIELD 4 CUPS

4	**RED ONIONS**
2 CUPS	**WATER** (DEPENDING ON SIZE OF BAKING PAN)
1 TBSP	**CHICKEN-FLAVORED CONSOMMÉ POWDER**

1 Peel and slice off the tops of the onions, leaving the root end intact. Using a melon baller, scoop out the inside of red onions and set aside for another use. Leave the outer two layers of each onion intact.

2 Place onions in an aluminum or glass baking pan. Add water and consommé powder. Bake, covered, for 30 minutes or until soft. Fill with orzo or mashed potatoes.

LO-MEIN NOODLES

PARVE

YIELD 4-6 SERVINGS

2 TBSP	**OLIVE OIL**
1	**ONION,** HALVED AND SLICED INTO THIN STRIPS
½	**RED BELL PEPPER,** SLICED INTO THIN STRIPS
½	**YELLOW BELL PEPPER,** SLICED INTO THIN STRIPS
½ CUP	**MUSHROOMS,** SLICED
½ CUP	**BEAN SPROUTS**
½ LB	**SPAGHETTI,** COOKED ACCORDING TO PACKAGE DIRECTIONS
3 TBSP	**SOY SAUCE**
3 TBSP	**THAI SWEET CHILI SAUCE** (SEE P. 80)

Can't find Thai sweet chili sauce? In Israel it's called *chili matok*. You can also substitute La Choy sweet and sour sauce, or make your own (see page 80).

My mother was not too happy when my sisters and I, dressed in cream gowns, stationed ourselves at the buffet at another sister's wedding. The attraction was this pasta, which was being made fresh. It was so addictive, it was worth the risk of a stain.

1 Heat olive oil in a sauté pan over medium heat. Add onion and cook for 1-2 minutes. Add peppers, mushrooms, and bean sprouts. Sauté for 4-5 minutes more until vegetables are slightly soft and lightly browned.

2 Add spaghetti, soy sauce, and sweet chili sauce. Cook for 2-3 minutes, stirring constantly.

SRIRACHA THAI NOODLES

PARVE

You can actually find kosher Thai-style noodles, but thin egg noodles work great in this recipe. Sriracha is a Thai-inspired hot sauce that adds great flavor.

1 Heat oil in large skillet. Sauté onion for a few minutes. Add carrots; cook for a few more minutes. Add zucchini, yellow squash, and mushrooms. Continue cooking for a few minutes, until vegetables are tender.

2 Add soy sauce and sriracha.

3 Cut scallions into long, thin strips. Place on top of vegetables, cover the skillet, and allow to steam for a minute or two.

4 Stir in the noodles. Serve hot.

YIELD 4-6 SERVINGS

3 TBSP	**OIL**
1 MEDIUM	**ONION,** THINLY DICED
1	**CARROT,** PEELED AND JULIENNED
2 SMALL	**ZUCCHINI,** PEELED AND JULIENNED
1 SMALL	**YELLOW SQUASH,** PEELED AND JULIENNED
8-10	**WHITE MUSHROOMS,** THINLY SLICED
3 TBSP	**SOY SAUCE**
1 TSP	**SRIRACHA**
1-2	**SCALLIONS**
12 OZ	**THIN EGG NOODLES,** COOKED ACCORDING TO PACKAGE DIRECTIONS

THE SHAPE OF IT ALL

Your kids tell you they don't like one shape of pasta and prefer one over another. And you say, "It's nonsense, they all taste the same." Not quite. Different shapes of pasta complement different sauces. Thin, delicate pastas, such as angel hair or thin spaghetti, should be served with light, thin sauces. Thicker pasta shapes, such as fettuccine, work well with heavier sauces. Pasta shapes with holes or ridges, such as ziti, are perfect for chunky sauces.

PENNE Penne complements virtually every sauce. It pairs exceptionally well with chunky meat, chunky vegetable, cream, or oil-based sauces. The shape is also great for baked dishes.

ROTINI ("Spirals") — Rotini's twisted shape holds bits of meat, vegetables, and cheese, so it works well with salads and baked casseroles.

BOW TIES Farfalle — Bow Ties brighten any meal with their interesting shape. They're thick enough for a variety of sauces, and a perfect addition to a salad or soup recipe.

ELBOW MACARONI Elbows are a highly versatile shape that can be topped with any sauce, baked, or put in soups, salads, and stir-fry dishes. Elbow macaroni is traditionally used to make macaroni and cheese.

SPAGHETTI America's favorite shape, spaghetti is the perfect choice for nearly any sauce. It can be used to make casseroles or stir-fry dishes. Go beyond tomato sauce and find your favorite.

BRUNCH & LUNCH

SPINACH-TOMATO PENNE PASTA

YIELD 6 SERVINGS

2 TBSP	**OIL**
2	**MEDIUM ONIONS,** DICED
2 CLOVES	**GARLIC,** PEELED AND MINCED
1 LB	**FROZEN SPINACH,** THAWED AND DRAINED
5	**PLUM TOMATOES,** DICED
•	**SALT AND PEPPER,** TO TASTE
2 CUPS	**HEAVY CREAM**
¼ CUP	**MOZZARELLA CHEESE,** SHREDDED
1 LB	**PENNE PASTA,** COOKED ACCORDING TO PACKAGE DIRECTIONS

This is a gourmet treat that's simple to make and will even convince your children (or husband) to eat spinach.

1 Heat the oil in a sauté pan over medium heat. Add the onion and garlic; cook until onion is soft.

2 Squeeze excess liquid from spinach.

3 Add the spinach and tomatoes and cook for 6-7 minutes, or until the mixture is soft. Season with salt and pepper. Lower heat; add the heavy cream and grated cheese and cook for 2-3 minutes.

4 Combine the sauce with the pasta and serve warm.

EGGPLANT & TOMATO FETTUCCINI

YIELD 6 SERVINGS

1	**MEDIUM EGGPLANT**
1½ CUPS	**CHERRY** OR **GRAPE TOMATOES**
5 TBSP	**OLIVE OIL, DIVIDED**
•	**SALT AND PEPPER,** TO TASTE
1 LB	**FETTUCCINI,** PREPARED ACCORDING TO PACKAGE DIRECTIONS

CREAM SAUCE (DAIRY)

2 CUPS	**HEAVY CREAM**
¾ CUP	**MOZZARELLA CHEESE,** SHREDDED
¼ TSP	**SALT**
½ TSP	**ITALIAN SEASONING**
•	**PINCH BLACK PEPPER**

OLIVE OIL DRESSING (PARVE)

½ CUP	**OLIVE OIL**
2 CLOVES	**GARLIC,** PEELED AND MINCED
½ TSP	**ITALIAN SEASONING**

Everyone can always use a new pasta idea for supper. This is superb because it works with both a heavy cream or an olive oil-based sauce. Sometimes I divide the pasta and toss each half with a different sauce to please all palates.

1 Preheat oven to 450°F.

2 Wash eggplant and dice into ½-inch cubes. Place on a baking sheet lined with parchment paper. Drizzle with 4 Tablespoons olive oil; season with salt and pepper. Bake on the top rack of the oven for 30 minutes.

3 Slice the tomatoes in half and place on a baking sheet lined with parchment paper. Drizzle with 1 Tablespoon olive oil and season with salt and pepper. Bake on the top rack of the oven for 12 minutes.

4 Combine the roasted vegetables with the cooked fettuccini.

5 To prepare the cream sauce, combine the cream, cheese, salt, seasoning, and pepper in a saucepan. Bring to a simmer; cook for 5 minutes. Adjust seasoning to taste.

6 To prepare the olive-oil dressing, combine the oil, garlic, and Italian seasoning.

7 Toss pasta with the sauce of your choice and adjust seasoning to taste. Serve warm.

PENNE WITH LEMON CREAM SAUCE

YIELD 2 SERVINGS

3 TBSP	**BUTTER**
1 CLOVE	**GARLIC,** PEELED AND CRUSHED
•	**JUICE OF ONE LEMON**
1¼ CUPS	**HEAVY CREAM**
3 TBSP	**PARMESAN CHEESE,** GRATED
1¼ TSP	**DRIED BASIL**
½ LB	**PENNE PASTA,** COOKED ACCORDING TO PACKAGE DIRECTIONS
•	**SALT AND PEPPER,** TO TASTE

Why a half-pound of pasta? I cook one pound of pasta and leave half for picky children who simply want to eat their pasta with ketchup! This sauce works best with penne — the pasta shape is so versatile, it'll go well with either a creamy sauce like this or a chunkier variety. You can also use fettuccini, but avoid spaghetti, as it won't hold this particular sauce well.

1   Melt the butter in a medium sauce pan over medium heat. Add the crushed garlic. Sauté for a few minutes, taking care not to burn it. Add the lemon juice (add only 2 Tablespoons of lemon juice if you don't like it so lemony) and stir. Add heavy cream. Simmer for 5 minutes. Add the parmesan cheese. Stir until cheese is melted. Season with basil.

2   Add the pasta and toss well. Season with salt and pepper.

3   If pasta is prepared in advance, reserve 3 Tablespoons of sauce to add while reheating.

4   Serve with additional parmesan cheese if desired.

NOTE

I'm all for store-bought lemon juice — up to a point. It's fine for lemonade (we don't want to have too many lemons to squeeze), or for a quick salad dressing. But when using lemon to add flavor to a delicate dish such as this pasta, use only fresh. Bottled lemon juice is too strong for the cream sauce.

ROASTED RED PEPPER CREAM PASTA

YIELD 4 SERVINGS

2-3	**LARGE RED BELL PEPPERS**
2 TBSP	**OIL**
1	**MEDIUM ONION,** DICED
3 CLOVES	**GARLIC,** PEELED AND CRUSHED
•	**SALT AND PEPPER,** TO TASTE
1 CUP	**HEAVY CREAM**
1 TBSP	**PARMESAN CHEESE.** GRATED + ADDITIONAL FOR SPRINKLING
¼ TSP	**DRIED BASIL**
1 LB	**PENNE PASTA,** COOKED ACCORDING TO PACKAGE DIRECTIONS
•	**FRESH BASIL LEAVES,** CHOPPED FOR GARNISH, OPTIONAL

I love roasted red peppers. When I was browsing the menu in a local restaurant and saw "Roasted Red Pepper Cream Pasta," I knew that's what I was ordering. They didn't have it that night, of course. A week or two later, I called the restaurant and asked if the pasta was available now. No, they answered, they did not have it. Enough of a wait. Why don't I just make the pasta myself?

1   Preheat oven to 475°F.

2   Place whole red bell peppers in oven and roast for 30 minutes, turning over once (the skin of the pepper should blister and blacken). Remove the peppers from the oven and transfer to a plastic bag. Allow peppers to "sweat" as they cool. When the peppers are cool enough to handle, remove from the bag. Remove and discard the stem, pith, and seeds. Peel off and discard the outer layer of the pepper.

3   In a blender or food processor, blend red peppers until smooth.

4   Heat the oil in a saucepan over medium heat. Add the onion and garlic; cook until the onion is soft. Add blended peppers, salt, and pepper. Add heavy cream and bring to a boil. Quickly lower heat. Add parmesan cheese and basil. Cook until sauce thickens.

5   Pour sauce over pasta; toss to coat. Top with additional parmesan cheese and fresh basil.

GOES WITH

22 | French Onion
Soup

PISTACHIO CREAMY BOW-TIE PASTA

DAIRY

YIELD 6 SIDE DISH SERVINGS

3-4 TBSP	**OLIVE OIL**
1	**MEDIUM ONION,** DICED
½ CUP	**PISTACHIOS,** CHOPPED
1¼ CUPS	**HEAVY CREAM**
•	**SALT AND PEPPER,** TO TASTE
1 LB	**FARFALLE** (BOW-TIE PASTA), COOKED ACCORDING TO PACKAGE DIRECTIONS

This is delicious, but is too heavy to serve as a main dish. Serve on a buffet or as a side with fish.

1 Heat the olive oil in a saucepot. Add the onion and cook until translucent. Add the pistachios and cook for 1 minute. Add the heavy cream. Bring to a boil, lower heat, and simmer for 5 minutes. Season with salt* and pepper.

2 Toss the sauce and pasta immediately before serving.

*If you use salted pistachios, you may not need salt.

LEEK & CHEESE CREPES

YIELD 12 SERVINGS

CREPES

2 CUPS	FLOUR
3	EGGS
1 CUP	MILK
2 TBSP	OIL
1 CUP	WATER
•	OIL OR BUTTER, FOR FRYING

LEEK-CHEESE FILLING

3 TBSP	BUTTER, DIVIDED
5	LEEKS, THINLY SLICED, WHITE AND LIGHT GREEN PARTS ONLY
4 CLOVES	GARLIC, PEELED AND MINCED
2 CUPS	COTTAGE CHEESE
1 CUP	MOZZARELLA CHEESE, GRATED
•	SALT AND PEPPER, TO TASTE
2	EGG YOLKS

Over the years, I've discovered some of my favorite recipes in other people's personal cookbooks, which are usually a selection gathered from numerous relatives and friends. One day, I "stole" my neighbor's book to find some new ideas and found this gem.

1 To prepare crepes, combine flour and eggs. Slowly whisk in the milk. Add oil and water gradually, whisking well until smooth. Refrigerate for a minimum of 2 hours.

2 Heat a 12-inch nonstick skillet over medium-high heat. Lightly coat the surface with oil or butter. Add ¼ cup batter, moving your wrist in a circular motion to coat the pan with a thin even layer. Cook for 1 minute or until the bottom browns lightly. Flip crepe and cook on the other side. Remove from pan.

3 Melt 2 Tablespoons butter in a skillet over medium heat. Add the leek and garlic; cook until soft and golden. Remove from heat. Stir in cheeses. Season with salt and pepper. Add yolks to mixture and mix well. Fill crepes blintz style or fold each filled crepe into a triangle. ▶

CHUNKY TOMATO SAUCE

2 TBSP	**OIL**
½ CUP	**SCALLIONS,** WHITE AND LIGHT GREEN PARTS ONLY, CHOPPED
4 CLOVES	**GARLIC,** PEELED AND MINCED
1 LB	**PLUM TOMATOES,** CHOPPED
1 CUP	**PARVE CHICKEN BROTH** (SEE P. 26)
¼ CUP	**WHITE WINE**
1	**BAY LEAF**
4 TBSP	**BUTTER**

4   Melt 1 Tablespoon butter in a skillet over medium heat. Add filled crepes and cook on both sides until golden. Keep warm.

5   To prepare Chunky Tomato Sauce, heat oil in a medium saucepan over medium heat. Add scallions and garlic and cook until tender. Add chopped tomatoes, broth, wine, bay leaf, and butter. Simmer for ½ hour. Discard bay leaf. Cook until sauce is reduced to 2 cups. Season with salt and pepper.

6   Serve crepes with Chunky Tomato Sauce.

AVOCADO & ROASTED PEPPER SANDWICH

YIELD 2 SERVINGS

1	**RED BELL PEPPER**
2	**SMALL BAGUETTES**
1	**AVOCADO,** SLICED
½	**MEDIUM RED ONION,** SLICED
½ CUP	**LETTUCE,** SHREDDED

DRESSING

½ CUP	**MAYONNAISE**
3 TBSP	**VINEGAR**
2 TBSP	**SUGAR**
2 TBSP	**WATER**
2 CLOVES	**GARLIC,** PEELED AND MINCED
•	**SALT AND PEPPER,** TO TASTE

The sandwich's simple, but the sublime taste is all about the great flavor combinations. You can serve it with your favorite dressing if you prefer.

1 Preheat oven to 475°F.

2 Place whole red bell pepper into oven and roast for 30 minutes, turning once (the skin of the pepper should blister and blacken). Remove the pepper from the oven and transfer it to a plastic bag. Allow pepper to "sweat" as it cools. When the pepper is cool enough to handle, remove it from the bag. Remove and discard the stem, pith, and seeds. Peel off and discard the outer layer of the pepper.

3 Combine all dressing ingredients and whisk until smooth.

4 Slice open each baguette. Layer on avocado, pepper, onion, and lettuce on one half of each baguette. Pour dressing over vegetables. Top with second half of baguette.

SPINACH GRILLED CHEESE

YIELD 5-6 SERVINGS

1 LOAF	**FRENCH BAGUETTE**
1-1 ½ CUPS	**MOZZARELLA AND CHEDDAR CHEESE,** SHREDDED

CREAMED SPINACH

2 TBSP	**OIL**
1	**SMALL ONION,** DICED
2 CLOVES	**GARLIC,** PEELED AND CRUSHED
1 LB	**FROZEN SPINACH,** THAWED AND DRAINED
1 CUP	**HEAVY CREAM**
•	**SALT AND PEPPER,** TO TASTE

This is an adult version of classic grilled cheese.

1 Preheat oven or toaster to 350°F.

2 To prepare creamed spinach, squeeze excess liquid from thawed spinach. Heat oil in a large sauté pan over medium heat. Add onion and garlic, sauté for 5 minutes or until soft. Add the spinach and cook for 2 minutes. Add the heavy cream, lower heat, and cook for 8-10 minutes or until sauce is reduced and mixture is creamy. Season with salt and pepper to taste.

3 Slice baguette into 1-inch slices. Top with a Table-spoon of creamed spinach and sprinkle with cheese. Place on baking sheet lined with parchment paper. Bake for 10 minutes, or until cheese melts.

4 Serve warm.

NOTE

Creamed spinach is also delicious on its own and over mashed potatoes or bow-tie pasta.

GOES WITH

22 | French Onion Soup

BAKED BASIL FRIES

YIELD 4 SERVINGS

4	**POTATOES,** WITH PEEL (RED OR YUKON GOLD)
•	**BOILING WATER,** TO COVER
2-3 TBLS	**OLIVE OIL**
¼ CUP	**GRATED PARMESAN CHEESE**
½ TSP	**GARLIC POWDER**
2 TBLS	**FRESH BASIL,** CHOPPED
•	**OIL,** TO GREASE PAN

Everyone can always use another way to prepare the humble spud. With basil and Parmesan cheese, what's there not to like in this version? Soaking the fries in hot water begins the baking process and results in crispy fries with a softer interior after baking. They're really perfect fries. If you like to dip your fries, prepare Garlic Mayonnaise (page 82) for a perfect accompaniment.

1 Position a rack in the center of the oven. Preheat oven to 450°F.

2 Wash and scrub the potatoes well. Cut into ¼-inch-thick sticks. Place into a large bowl. Pour boiling water over the fries. Let sit for 10-25 minutes. Drain and pat dry. Toss with the oil, cheese, garlic, and basil.

3 Grease a baking sheet well. Spread fries on the pan in one layer.

4 Bake for 20 minutes. Flip fries over and bake an additional 20-30 minutes.

NOTE

The heavier the baking sheet, the faster the fries will bake.

FALAFEL

1 LB	**DRIED GARBANZO BEANS** (CHICKPEAS)
•	**WATER,** FOR SOAKING
1 HEAD	**GARLIC,** PEELED (12-14 CLOVES)
1	**MEDIUM ONION,** QUARTERED
3	**EGGS**
2 TBSP	**DRIED CILANTRO LEAVES**
1 TSP	**BLACK PEPPER**
1 SCANT TBSP	**SALT**
1 TBSP	**BAKING SODA**
1 TBSP	**GROUND CUMIN**
2 TBSP	**FLOUR**
1¾-2 CUP	**WATER**
1 CUP	**BREADCRUMBS** (OR MORE AS NEEDED)
•	**OIL,** FOR FRYING

Why is falafel so popular in Israel? I tried polling falafel shop owners to find out. One told me to "just taste it" and I'd understand why people flock to his stand. A more humble owner told me he's in the best location. When I asked taxi drivers their opinion on the best falafel in town, each offered to drive me to his favorite spot — one "best falafel stand" was two hours away! Though falafel is Israel's national food, most Israelis do not attempt to make it at home. Why should they, when a typical falafel sandwich costs only 7 shekels?

Those who sell falafel usually own a secret recipe that has been passed down from father to son. One owner told me that he had bought his shop after serving in the army. The previous owner was ready to retire, and with the recipe included as part of the contract, the shop now offers the former soldier the means to support his family.

For those of you who live outside of Israel and yearn for that authentic falafel experience, here it is. Thanks to my Aunt Yenti for these. The recipe will yield about 75 balls, depending on size. Though by the time I'm done rolling and frying, many of the balls have already been eaten!

Leftover batter can be frozen for another time. Simply defrost and add a bit of breadcrumbs to the mixture to thicken before forming the balls.

1. Soak the chickpeas overnight in water. For a quicker soak, place chickpeas into a pot. Add water until the peas are submerged beneath two inches of liquid. Bring to a boil and cook for 2 minutes. Remove from heat. Cover and let stand for 1 hour. Drain.

2. In a food processor or with grinder, grind chickpeas, garlic, and onion. Place mixture into a large bowl. Stir in remaining ingredients. Refrigerate for a minimum of 30 minutes.

3. Fill a pot halfway with oil. Heat oil over medium-high heat. Form batter into tight balls with a small ice-cream scooper. Test-fry one ball; if it falls apart, add breadcrumbs. Slip balls into oil, a few at a time. Do not crowd. Fry until golden on all sides. Remove with a slotted spoon. Drain on paper towels.

NOTE

Some people might be tempted to take a shortcut and use canned chickpeas. This is a warning: canned chickpeas do not work here. They retain too much water and are too soft. Falafel made from canned chickpeas will be too mushy. The original recipe calls for fresh cilantro leaves. By using dried leaves, I can put together a batch of falafel from ingredients found in my pantry any day of the year.

GOES WITH

156 | Pita   70 | Techina   70 | Chunky Hummus

THE PERFECT PIZZA

Over the years, I've tried many recipes for pizza dough. Some were okay and others were passable. I gave up and resorted to buying pizza dough at my local pizza shop for $3 a piece (prices have gone up since then).

A few years ago, a pizza shop I frequented closed down. If there was one thing I actually liked about their pizza, it was their dough. The owner was retiring, so I figured I had nothing to lose, and I set out to nudge, plead, and shamelessly beg for the recipe. It took some convincing, but since his retirement was on the horizon, I finally succeeded.

The problem was that the recipe was all in percentages. 100% flour ... 1.8% salt. I placed the recipe on my desk, and it haunted me for months. I regretted the day I made the decision in eleventh grade to forgo calculus. Yet the urge to have the recipe took over, and late one night, I sat down with a calculator and broke down the recipe, bit by bit. Eureka! Some tweaking was done, and it was perfect. I then proceeded to tear up every other pizza dough recipe I had ever written down.

PIZZA DOUGH

YIELD 4 12-14-INCH
PIZZA PIES

2½ LB	**WHITE FLOUR** (SEE SIDEBAR)
1 TBSP	**SALT**
3 TBSP	**SUGAR**
2¼ TSP	**DRY YEAST**
3 CUPS	**WATER**
2 TBSP	**OIL**

1 Place all the dry ingredients into a large mixer bowl and combine at low speed for 10 seconds.

2 Add the water and mix on low for 2 minutes. Add the oil and mix on low for 2 minutes. Turn the mixer to high for an additional 2 minutes.

3 Divide dough into 4 balls. Coat each ball well with flour and cover with a kitchen towel. Let rise for 1½ hours.

4 If not using immediately, dough can be refrigerated or frozen by placing balls into individual plastic bags (coat with flour again to reduce stickiness). Bring to room temperature before using the dough.

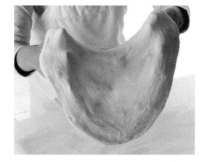

NOTE

MEASURING FLOUR

Weight and cup measurements of flour never equal each other. Eight cups of sifted flour is a lot less than 8 cups of unsifted flour. If you have a kitchen scale, measure out 2½ lbs of flour. Otherwise, use 7½ cups of unsifted flour and sift it afterward. If your flour is freshly sifted, pack it down. If you're a beginner baker, add up to an additional ½ cup of flour. Your dough will be more dense, but it will still taste quite good. If you are a more advanced baker, let the dough be sticky. Flour your hands and work surface well. You'll be rewarded with a light, airy dough.

MORE TO A BALL

When dividing your dough into balls, you want each one to be airtight. To accomplish this, flatten the ball into a small disk. Then, gather all the edges into a pouch. Hold the dough so that the gathered edges are in your right hand and the rounded side is in your left. Keep rotating and pulling the corners until you have a seamless ball and no air pockets.

MAKING YOUR PIZZA

YIELD 1 12" PIZZA

1 BALL	**PREPARED PIZZA DOUGH**
•	**CORNMEAL**
5-6 TBSP	**PIZZA SAUCE**
6 HANDFULS	**MOZZARELLA** OR **3-CHEESE PIZZA CHEESE**, SHREDDED

A combination of three cheeses — cheddar, mozzarella, and muenster — works well on pizza.

1 Preheat oven to 475°F.

2 Using only your hands and plenty of flour (no rolling pin) stretch and pull the dough until it forms a 12"-14" circle. Sprinkle cornmeal on parchment paper and place the dough on top. Spread with pizza sauce. Sprinkle with cheese; add more to taste. Trim off the extra paper.

3 Slide the pizza, with its paper, onto the preheated pizza stone. Bake for 13 minutes on the lowest rack of oven. Check the crust for readiness (it should be golden brown).

PIZZA SAUCE

YIELD 2 CUPS

1 16oz CAN	**TOMATO SAUCE**
¾ TSP	**GARLIC POWDER**
¾ TSP	**ITALIAN SEASONING**

The simplest, cheapest, and easiest pizza sauce is plain tomato sauce with spices. Alternatively, use equal parts water and tomato paste with a pinch of sugar. You can also substitute dried oregano for the Italian seasoning. If you refrigerate the sauce overnight, the texture will resemble bought pizza sauce.

• Combine all ingredients.

BAKING WITH A PIZZA STONE

If you or your family are pizza fans, it is worth investing in a pizza stone. They cost as little as $15, and some include a wooden pizza peel, just like the pros use. Pizza stones are flat, heavy, unglazed stones that usually come in either round or rectangular shapes. Their main advantage is that they help to distribute the heat of the oven evenly to your pizza or other baked goods. Their porous nature helps to absorb excess moisture, creating a crisper crust.

Here's how to use your pizza stone for best results:

- Place your pizza stone on the bottom rack of a cold oven.

- Preheat your stone in the oven on 475°F for a minimum of 30 minutes.

- Place your pizza dough on parchment paper sprinkled with cornmeal. Cut the extra paper off. This makes it easier to slide the pizza off the peel and on and off the baking stone.

- Leave the pizza stone to cool in the oven.

- When cool, clean stone using only clear, plain water, and let it air dry overnight.

THIN-CRUST PIZZA WITH RED WINE TOMATO SAUCE

YIELD 4 8-INCH INDIVIDUAL PIZZAS

3 CUPS	FLOUR, PACKED
1 CUP	WATER
2¼ TSP	DRY YEAST
1 TSP	SALT
1 TSP	SUGAR
1 TBSP	OIL
•	CORNMEAL, FOR DUSTING
•	MOZZARELLA OR PIZZA CHEESE, SHREDDED, FOR TOPPING

RED WINE TOMATO SAUCE

¼ CUP	TOMATO PASTE
¼ CUP	WATER
1 TBSP	RED WINE
1½ TSP	SUGAR
¼ TSP	SALT
¼ TSP	OREGANO

This is my quick version of pizza dough, for days when you're not about to make dough in bulk, and there's none left in your freezer. The trick to a good pizza is leaving the dough slightly sticky. If the dough is too heavy with flour, the crust will be dense, distracting from the flavor and texture of the final product. If you find the dough hard to handle, coat it with a light dusting of flour instead of incorporating more flour into the dough. The red wine tomato sauce is a bit more sophisticated than the standard pizza sauce. You can also prepare this dough by hand, using a wooden spoon.

1 Combine the flour, water, dry yeast, salt, and sugar in a mixing bowl. Mix on medium speed for 1-2 minutes. You may need to add 1-2 Tablespoons of water or flour if the dough is too wet or too dry, but don't add more than that. Add the oil and incorporate well into the dough.

2 Dust dough with flour and place into a bowl. Cover and allow to rise for 30 minutes.

3 While the dough is rising, thoroughly combine all the sauce ingredients. ▶

4   Preheat oven to 500°F.

5   Line 2 baking sheets with parchment paper. Dust each sheet with cornmeal.

6   Divide dough into 4 parts. Using a rolling pin, roll out each part to an 8-inch circle or as thin as possible.

7   Transfer 2 circles of dough onto each prepared baking sheet. Divide the tomato sauce between the pizza pies. Sprinkle with shredded cheese. Bake for 10-11 minutes or until ready.

NOTE

You may substitute ½ cup tomato sauce instead of the tomato paste and water. Adjust seasoning to taste.

Want to spice it up? Top pizza with additional vegetables, such as peppers, tomatoes, and onions, or skip the tomato sauce and cheese and finish it off with olive oil, garlic, and za'atar instead.

MUSHROOM CALZONES

YIELD 7 PERSONAL-SIZE CALZONES

1 BATCH	**PIZZA DOUGH** (BOUGHT OR HOMEMADE — ABOUT 2 LB.)(1½ BALLS OF RECIPE ON P. 144)
1	**MEDIUM ONION,** DICED
2 TBSP	**OIL**
10oz	**FRESH MUSHROOMS,** DICED
¼ TSP	**SALT**
•	**BLACK PEPPER** TO TASTE
¼ TSP + DASH	**OREGANO**
3oz	**CREAM CHEESE** (NOT WHIPPED)
½ CUP	**RICOTTA CHEESE**
1	**SCALLION,** WHITE AND LIGHT GREEN PARTS ONLY, THINLY SLICED
¾ CUP	**MOZZARELLA CHEESE,** SHREDDED
1	**EGG,** BEATEN
•	**MARINARE SAUCE,** OPTIONAL

1 Divide the dough into 7 parts. Set aside.

2 Heat oil in a frying pan over medium heat. Add the onion and cook for 2 minutes. Add the mushrooms and cook an additional 10 minutes. Season with salt, pepper, and oregano.

3 In a small bowl, combine the cream cheese, ricotta cheese, and scallion. Season with additional black pepper and dash of oregano. Set aside

4 Preheat oven to 450°F.

5 Working with one ball at a time, roll out dough into an 8-inch circle. Spread ½ of the cheese mixture over the circle, leaving at least a 1-inch border around the edge. Sprinkle mozzarella cheese on one half of the cheese. Top mozzarella with mushroom filling. Gently pull the other side of the circle over the filling, lining up the edges to form a half-moon shape. Press the edges together with the tines of a fork. Use a knife to trim any excess dough; you should have a neat half-circle.

6 For a decorative touch, use your index fingers to crimp the edges of the dough.

7 Repeat with the remaining dough and filling.

8 Transfer the filled calzones to a baking sheet lined with parchment paper. Cut one or two small slits into the top of each calzone. Brush the tops with beaten egg. Bake for 18-20 minutes or until golden brown.

9 Serve with marinara sauce, if desired.

GARLIC KNOTS

YIELD 30 MINI KNOTS

1½ LB	**PIZZA** OR **CHALLAH DOUGH,** OR 1 PACKAGE PURCHASED PIZZA DOUGH
¼ CUP	**OLIVE OIL**
6-8 CLOVES	**GARLIC,** PEELED AND MINCED
1 HEAPING TBSP	**PARSLEY FLAKES**
DASH	**SALT,** OPTIONAL

Many people believe that you make garlic knots by brushing the knots with oil and garlic before you bake them. The opposite is true. These are totally irresistible and taste way better than the variety you'd buy. While I prefer to make them with pizza dough, the recipe works well with challah dough, too.

For an exciting variation, replace the parsley with za'atar.

1 Preheat oven to 475°F. Line a baking sheet with parchment paper.

2 Roll out the dough to the size the baking sheet. Using a pizza cutter, cut the dough crosswise into thin strips. You should have about 15 strips. Cut each strip in half lengthwise. Tie each strip into a knot. Place on prepared baking sheet.

3 Bake for 7-9 minutes. Knots should be slightly browned with the bottoms still white (otherwise they will be too hard).

4 In a large bowl, combine olive oil, garlic, parsley, and salt, if using.

5 Toss warm baked knots with the olive oil mixture.

NOTE

THE MINCE VS. THE CRUSH

The way you chop garlic does affect the flavor. For this recipe, you need to mince. While you can easily crush garlic by using a press, minced garlic needs to be finely chopped with a knife or any one of a number of special kitchen gadgets created for the task.

ITALIAN STICKS

YIELD 2 SERVINGS

½ **PIZZA BALL** (⅛ OF THE PIZZA DOUGH RECIPE)

• **OIL,** FOR SMEARING

• **CORNMEAL**

• **ITALIAN SEASONING**

1 Place pizza stone into oven. Preheat to 475°F.

2 Oil the bottom and sides of a 10-inch round aluminum pan. Sprinkle generously with cornmeal. Using your fingertips, spread the dough into a 10-inch circle and place in the pan. Dimple the dough all over, using your index finger. Smear oil on top and sprinkle with Italian seasoning. Placing pan directly on a heated pizza stone, bake for 11-15 minutes.

3 Remove bread from pan. Using a pizza cutter, cut bread into 6-7 sticks. Serve immediately.

4 Serve with warmed marina or pizza sauce for dipping.

PITA

A good falafel deserves fresh pita — and it's simple to make your own, certainly easier than baking challos!

YIELD 8 PITAS

2¼ TSP	DRY YEAST
1¼ CUPS	WARM WATER
1 TBSP	SUGAR
3 CUPS	FLOUR
1½ TSP	SALT
2 TBSP	OIL

1 In a mixing bowl, place yeast, water, and sugar. Add the flour and mix for 30 seconds. Add salt and oil. Mix on medium speed for 8-10 minutes. If the dough looks too dry, add up to an additional ¼ cup water if necessary.

2 Lightly coat a bowl with oil and place the dough inside. Cover the bowl with plastic wrap or a damp towel. Let rise 1½ hours. When the dough has doubled, punch down and divide dough into 8 pieces. Roll each part into a ball. Cover with a damp towel or plastic wrap and let rest for 20 minutes.

3 Meanwhile, center a rack in the oven and insert an inverted baking sheet or pizza stone.

4 Preheat the oven to 425°F.

5 Lightly coat your working surface with flour. Using a rolling pin, roll out the balls of dough to 6-inch circles. Lightly dust both sides with flour. If you have trouble rolling out the dough, let it rest an additional 10 minutes and try again. Cover the dough circles until ready to bake so they don't dry out.

6 Throw 2 ice cubes into the bottom of the oven, and place 3 dough circles on top of the inverted baking sheet. Bake for 4-5 minutes. Pita should puff up. Remove carefully and let cool. Repeat with remaining dough.

NOTE

The ice cubes melt and fill the oven with steam, allowing the pitas to stay moist. This ensures that the outside doesn't dry out before the insides puff up.

GOES WITH

140 | Falalafel

192 | Chicken Fajitas

GRILLED FLATBREAD

YIELD 8 FLATBREADS

1 TSP	SUGAR
2¾ TSP	DRY YEAST
1 CUP	WARM WATER
3 CUPS	FLOUR
2 TSP	SALT
1 TSP	ITALIAN SEASONING
•	OIL, FOR BRUSHING

You don't need to save your grill pan for the main dish only. Use it for side dishes and bread too. Nothing rounds out a meal like fresh bread. These are quick, easy, and fun to prepare!

1 Combine the sugar, yeast, and water. Let sit 2 minutes. Add in the flour, salt, and Italian seasoning. Mix well to combine. (I don't add in all the flour at once. Add most of it and then add as much as you need to form a good dough.) Cover and let rise 1 hour in a greased bowl.

2 Divide the dough into 8 pieces. Roll each piece as thin as you can, about 6 to 8 inches wide. It doesn't have to be a pretty circle as long as the dough is an even thickness.

3 Heat a grill pan over high heat for 5 minutes.

4 Brush one side of the dough with oil and place oil side down on the pan. While bread is grilling, brush the upper side with oil. Flip over and bake on the other side. Continue with remaining dough.

GOES WITH_____

178 | Rosemary
Chicken Cutlets

DOUBLE CHOCOLATE PECAN WAFFLES

YIELD 12 WAFFLES

1½ CUPS	FLOUR
1 CUP	SUGAR
2 TBSP	VANILLA SUGAR
1 TBSP	BAKING POWDER
3 TBSP	COCOA, SIFTED
¼ TSP	SALT
½ CUP	OIL
2	EGGS
1¼ CUPS	MILK
1 TSP	CHOCOLATE LIQUOR
½ CUP	CHOCOLATE CHIPS OR ½-BAR (1.5oz) BITTERSWEET CHOCOLATE, CHOPPED
½ CUP	CHOPPED PECANS
½ CUP	COCOA CRISPIES CEREAL, OPTIONAL

1 Lightly coat the inside of a waffle iron with nonstick cooking spray or wipe with a paper towel lightly coated with oil.

2 In a large bowl, combine flour, sugars, baking powder, cocoa, and salt. Stir to combine. Add oil, eggs, milk, and chocolate liquor to form a batter. Pour approximately ¼-cup batter into waffle maker, following manufacturer's instructions. Do not fill the entire mold as the waffle will expand as it cooks.

3 Sprinkle some chocolate chips, chopped pecans, and Cocoa Crispies cereal (if using) on top of waffle and close the waffle maker.

4 The waffle maker will signal when the waffles are ready. Waffles should be lightly browned and crisp.

ICED MOCHA COFFEE

YIELD 8-10 SERVINGS

8½ CUPS	**MILK** (2 LITERS OR A ½ GALLON + ½ CUP)
2 TBSP	**INSTANT COFFEE GRANULES**
¼ CUP	**BOILING WATER**
½ TSP	**VANILLA SUGAR**
½ CUP	**SUGAR**
2 TSP	**CHOCOLATE SYRUP**
1 TBSP	**CHOCOLATE LIQUOR**

Want to recreate those iced coffees you buy in cafes? This is not just a regular iced coffee with a couple of ice cubes, but an authentic slush. Rivky Rubin, a young girl who will be a fantastic cook one day, made these for a kiddush on Shabbos morning, and the whole neighborhood finished them to the last drop. You might need extra defrost time, so plan ahead.

1   Combine all ingredients in a pitcher. Freeze overnight.

2   Defrost 4-6 hours prior to serving. Mix well, smashing clumps of ice, and serve.

STRAWBERRY SMOOTHIE

1 CUP	**ORANGE JUICE**
½ CUP	**SUGAR**
1 LB	**FROZEN STRAWBERRIES**
1½ CUP	**MILK**
½ CUP	**DESSERT WINE**
DASH	**VANILLA SUGAR**

1   Blend orange juice, sugar, and frozen strawberries until smooth. Freeze.

2   Defrost until mixture is slushy. Add milk, dessert wine, and vanilla sugar. Stir well.

POTS AND PANS

Throughout this cookbook, I've stuck to the basics, referring to the types of pots and pans that most people have in their kitchen. We've fried in a skillet, boiled in a saucepan, and cooked complete dishes in a sauté pan. For those with an expanded pot-and-pan repertoire, make use of your wok for those stir-fries and your grill pan for hamburgers.

SAUCE POT

GRILL PAN

WOK

SKILLET

SAUTÉ PAN

MAIN DISHES

HONEY-MUSTARD CHICKEN

YIELD 3-4 SERVINGS

1½ LB	**CHICKEN CUTLETS**
⅛ TSP	**SALT**
⅛ TSP	**PEPPER**
3-4 TBSP	**OIL**
2	**LARGE ONIONS,** DICED
•	**VEGETABLES,** OPTIONAL
3 TBSP	**HONEY**
3 TBSP	**SOY SAUCE**
3 TBSP	**MUSTARD**

Sometimes I go through recipe phases. I'll get hooked on one and make it again and again, until a new recipe enters the repertoire for the next couple of months. This is one of the recipes that's currently a staple in my house. It's so quick and easy, no wonder I've been making it over and over!

In the photo, you'll notice strips of red and yellow peppers. This recipe is so versatile, though, you can use any produce that's in season or sitting in your vegetable drawer — or none at all! See page 177 for suggestions on stir-fry additions. One ingredient you can't skip, though, are those onions. They get sautéed to the most delicious caramelized goodness that I often add an additional onion to the recipe so peace will reign at my supper table.

1 Cut chicken cutlets into 2-inch strips. Season with salt and pepper.

2 Heat the oil in a large frying pan over medium heat. Add onion and cook for 10-15 minutes or until golden brown.

3 Add chicken strips and cook for 5 minutes. Add vegetables, if using.

4 Add honey, mustard, and soy sauce. Cook for 10-15 minutes (stirring occasionally), or until sauce reduces. Serve over orzo or rice.

CRISPY CHICKEN FINGERS WITH DIPPING SAUCE

YIELD 4 SERVINGS

1½ LB	**CHICKEN CUTLETS**
1 CLOVE	**GARLIC,** PEELED AND CRUSHED
⅛ TSP	**PAPRIKA**
1	**EGG,** BEATEN
1-2 CUPS	**PANKO CRUMBS** (SEE SIDEBAR)
•	**OIL,** FOR FRYING

These are the crispiest chicken cutlets you will ever meet. If you prefer cornflake crumbs over breadcrumbs, you'll love panko crumbs.

My personal favorite is to serve these with the buffalo sauce. It's a definite winner, especially for men who enjoy their food with a real kick. You can adjust the pepper seasoning for more or less heat. One thing to look out for: every brand of hot sauce tastes a little different, so you may need to taste the sauce ahead of time and adjust the seasonings.

1 Pound chicken cutlets until they are ⅓-inch thick. Cut into long strips. Season strips with crushed garlic and paprika.

2 Dip the chicken into egg, then into panko crumbs. Heat oil in a skillet or frying pan and fry strips on both sides until crisp and golden.

3 Serve chicken with your choice of dipping sauce.

4 To prepare buffalo sauce, combine all ingredients in a saucepan and bring to a boil. Remove from heat.

5 To prepare creamy hot sauce, combine chili sauce, honey, sugar, and water in a medium pot. Bring to a boil. Lower flame to a simmer and add Thousand Island dressing. Remove from heat.

BUFFALO SAUCE

½ CUP	CAYENNE PEPPER SAUCE OR HOT SAUCE
¼ CUP	HONEY
1½ TBSP	SUGAR
1 TBSP	VINEGAR
¼ TSP	GROUND RED PEPPER OR CAYENNE PEPPER (PAPRIKA CHARIFA)
•	DASH OF PAPRIKA

CREAMY HOT SAUCE

¼ CUP	CHILI SAUCE
¼ CUP	HONEY
1 TBSP	SUGAR
2 TSP	WATER
½ CUP	THOUSAND ISLAND DRESSING

GOES WITH

96 | Dijon Red Potato Wedges

93 | Sunflower Green Beans

NOTE

PANKO

Panko is a breadcrumb originating in Japanese cuisine. It's lighter, crispier, and crunchier than Western bread crumbs. Since the crumbs are coarsely ground, panko looks more like flakes than like crumbs, enabling them to stay crispier longer and absorb less grease. The crumbs have a large surface area and seasonings adhere well to them.

To make panko crumbs, push chunks of day-old white bread through the shredding disk of your food processor to form coarse crumbs. Place on a baking sheet and bake at 300°F for 6-8 minutes until dry but not toasted. Let cool. Panko will keep in the freezer for months.

TERIYAKI SESAME CHICKEN

Everybody loves sesame chicken, but every recipe I see inevitably includes ketchup. The restaurants, though, do not use ketchup. I wanted to make sesame chicken the authentic way, with purely Asian flavors and no American condiments. This chicken is not red, but it is genuine.

YIELD 8 SERVINGS

BATTER

¾ CUP	**CORNSTARCH**
¾ CUP	**FLOUR**
2 TSP	**BAKING POWDER**
1 TSP	**BAKING SODA**
1 CUP	**COLD WATER**
3 LB	**CHICKEN CUTLETS,** CUT INTO NUGGETS
2 CUPS	**OIL**

SAUCE

1 CUP	**SUGAR**
½ CUP	**BROWN-RICE VINEGAR**
6 TBSP	**SOY SAUCE**
6 CLOVES	**GARLIC,** PEELED AND CRUSHED
2 TBSP	**SESAME OIL**
6 TBSP	**WATER**
2 TBSP	**CORNSTARCH**
•	**TOASTED SESAME SEEDS**

1 Combine the batter ingredients.

2 Heat 2 cups of oil in a wok for 10 minutes. Dip the chicken nuggets into the batter and ad to wok. Fry until they are golden brown and cooked through. Drain the chicken on a paper towel and place into a 9x13-inch pan.

3 Combine the sugar, vinegar, soy sauce, garlic, and sesame oil in a small pot over high heat. Stir and bring to a boil. Combine water and cornstarch and add to pot. Cook until sauce thickens.

4 Pour sauce over chicken. Sprinkle with sesame seeds.

5 To reheat, bake, uncovered, for 10 minutes at 350°F.

GOES WITH

114 | Couscous With Vegetables

119 | Sriracha Thai Noodles

ASIAN-INSPIRED CHICKEN STRIPS

YIELD 4 SERVINGS

- **OIL,** FOR FRYING
- 4 **CHICKEN CUTLETS,** CUT INTO STRIPS
- 3 **EGG WHITES**
- **CORNSTARCH,** FOR DREDGING
- 2 TBSP **MUSTARD**
- 6 TBSP **SUGAR**
- 4 TBSP **SOY SAUCE**
- 3 TBSP **SESAME OIL**
- 4 TBSP **VINEGAR**

Dipping the chicken into cornstarch and then egg whites makes for an exceptionally crunchy, succulent chicken. Topped with an Asian-inspired sauce, it's a delicious supper that's only good fresh out of the pan. Serve with Lo-Mein Noodles (page 118) or over rice with a side of roasted vegetables.

1 Heat the oil in a frying pan over medium-high heat.

2 Place the egg whites into a small bowl. With a hand whisk or two forks, beat the egg whites until frothy.

3 Coat the chicken strips with cornstarch. Dip into the beaten egg whites and fry on both sides until crispy and golden. Transfer to a plate lined with paper towels. You will need to re-beat the egg whites often as you work.

4 Pour off the remaining oil that is in the pan. To the pan, add the mustard, sugar, soy sauce, oil, and vinegar. Cook for 1-2 minutes until the sauce is smooth. Return the chicken strips to the pan and stir gently until they are well coated and sauce clings to chicken. Serve immediately.

GOES WITH_____

118 | Lo-Mein Noodles

SWEET BUFFALO CHICKEN

BUFFALO SAUCE

⅓ CUP	**HOT SAUCE** (SUCH AS FRANK'S BRAND)
½ CUP	**BROWN SUGAR**
½ CUP	**SUGAR**
¼ CUP	**HONEY**

CHICKEN NUGGETS

1 CUP	**FLOUR**
3 TBSP	**BREAD CRUMBS**
1 TBSP	**PAPRIKA**
1 TBSP	**OREGANO**
1 TSP	**SALT**
1-1½ LB	**CHICKEN CUTLETS** CUT INTO NUGGETS
1 CUP	**LEMON LIME SODA**

CHICKEN WINGS

1 LB	**CHICKEN WINGS**
1 TSP	**PAPRIKA**
•	**SALT AND PEPPER,** TO TASTE

I can't vouch that it tastes the same, but rumor has it that this is similar to a restaurant's hot sauce. Serve with chicken nuggets as a dipping sauce, or use as a marinade for the wings.

1   To prepare Buffalo Sauce, combine all sauce ingredients in a medium saucepan. Bring to a boil, reduce heat, and simmer until sauce is smooth, stirring occasionally.

2   To prepare chicken nuggets, combine flour, breadcrumbs, and seasonings in a small bowl. Set aside. Marinate chicken nuggets in soda for a few minutes. Dip each piece of chicken in breading. In a deep fryer or in a pot over medium heat, fry chicken until batter is light brown and crisp. Drain on paper towels.

3   Serve sauce alongside nuggets as a dip.

4   To prepare chicken wings, place wings into a baking dish and season with paprika, salt, and pepper. Pour sauce over wings and bake for 40 minutes in an oven preheated to 425°F. Then broil for 5 minutes and serve with Buffalo Sauce.

GOES WITH_____

42 | Cucumber Salad

92 | Squash Soufflés

CHICKEN STIR FRY

2 TBSP	**OIL**
¾ LB	**CHICKEN CUTLETS,** CUT INTO THIN STRIPS
1	**LARGE ONION,** CUT INTO NARROW WEDGES
1	**LARGE RED BELL PEPPER,** CUT INTO THIN STRIPS
2	**CARROTS,** JULIENNED
½ CUP	**SUGAR-SNAP PEAS**

STIR FRY SAUCE

3 TBSP	**SOY SAUCE**
1 TBSP	**VINEGAR**
1 CLOVE	**GARLIC,** PEELED AND CRUSHED
2 TSP	**SUGAR**
4 TSP	**CORNSTARCH**
⅔ CUP	**WATER**
•	**SALT AND PEPPER** TO TASTE

OPTIONAL GARNISH

•	**WONTON WRAPPERS**
•	**OIL,** FOR FRYING

I remember one of the first times I made stir fry. I followed the directions in the cookbook to a "T." If that meant going to two different stores to buy all the ingredients, I did. Today, I laugh at myself. Stir fries are a supper when I have five minutes to cook, and I want to use all the produce I have in my vegetable drawer ... or it's for when my children are eating leftovers and I don't want to (one of the perks of adulthood). If you prefer baby corn instead of sugar-snap peas, switch it. Add more bell peppers or use only chicken and carrots — whatever you want! To make a delicious stir fry, all you need are fresh ingredients (forget about frozen vegetable mixes) and a good sauce.

1 Heat the oil in a large wok over high heat. Add the chicken strips and sauté for 4-6 minutes, stirring until the chicken whitens. Remove chicken from the pan and set aside.

2 Add the onion to the wok and sauté until slightly soft. Add the pepper and cook for 2 minutes. Add the carrots and the sugar-snap peas and cook for 1-2 minutes.

3 Combine all the sauce ingredients in a medium bowl.

4 Return the chicken to the wok. Add the sauce. (See note on facing page.) Cook for 4-5 minutes, stirring occasionally, until sauce thickens. Serve immediately.

5 To garnish, cut wonton wrappers into thin strips and deep fry in hot oil in a small pot for 30-60 seconds. Drain on a paper towel and serve over the stir fry.

NOTE

TIPS TO MAKE A PERFECT STIR FRY

- Start with a large wok so that the ingredients have room to cook. While you can use a large skillet, the sloped sides of a wok are ideal for quick and even cooking.
- Cut all vegetables into pieces that are the same size.
- Prepare the sauce.
- Stir fry according to density, with the densest vegetables being stir fried for the longest time.
- Some people like their vegetables nice and crunchy, and others like them completely cooked through and soft. Use your instinct to decide how long to cook the vegetables.
- When adding sauce to the wok, form a "well" in the middle, pushing the vegetables and chicken to the sides. Add the sauce to the middle and stir to thicken before mixing with the rest of the ingredients.
- Serve fresh out of the pan.

GREAT VEGGIES FOR A STIR FRY

Red bell peppers • Yellow bell peppers • Sugar-snap peas • Onions • Baby corn • Bamboo shoots/Mung sprouts • Water chestnuts • Carrots • Mushrooms

ADDITIONS TO JAZZ IT UP

Sesame seeds • Cashews or any other nuts • Cooked pasta

While filleting chicken, freeze the extra little pieces of the cutlets in a bag. Next time you make a stir fry, you'll have ready-made little nuggets.

ROSEMARY CHICKEN CUTLETS

YIELD 3-4 SERVINGS

1 TSP	**ROSEMARY**
1 TSP	**OREGANO**
1 TSP	**GROUND CUMIN**
1 TSP	**PAPRIKA**
½ TSP	**SALT**
¼ TSP	**BLACK PEPPER**
2 TBSP	**OLIVE OIL**
1 – 1½ LB.	**BREAST** OR **DARK MEAT CHICKEN CUTLETS,** POUNDED THIN AND SLICED INTO STRIPS

BBQ WHITE SAUCE

¾ CUP	**MAYONNAISE**
2 TBSP	**VINEGAR**
1 CLOVE	**GARLIC,** PEELED AND CRUSHED
½ TSP	**PEPPER**
½ TSP	**SPICY BROWN MUSTARD**
½ TSP	**SUGAR**
½ TSP	**SALT**

I used to hate grilling indoors. Then I discovered grill pans. They're not perfect (there's no charcoal taste), but the results are so close to what an outdoor grill can achieve that I've become rather attached to them. I baby my grill pan and now favor it over anything else in the pot drawer — if it can barbeque in the winter, it's a must-have for me.

These cutlets are full of flavor. Pound the chicken thin and you'll be rewarded with juicy meat that will keep you from counting down the days until the snow melts from around your outdoor grill.

1 Combine the rosemary, oregano, cumin, paprika, salt, and pepper. Mix with the olive oil and rub onto chicken to coat well. Marinate 30 minutes (or up to 6 hours) in the refrigerator.

2 Spray a grill pan with cooking spray. Preheat the grill pan over high heat for a full 5 minutes.

3 Discard marinade. Place chicken on pan. When most of the chicken is white, turn the chicken over and cook for an additional 1-2 minutes. To achieve grill marks, do not move chicken while cooking. Be careful not to overcook.

4 Whisk all sauce ingredients together. Serve over cutlets.

NOTE

FAST IDEAS FOR A RANGE OF FLAVORS

Want to change up the flavor a bit? Try these combinations for winning spice rubs and marinades:

- Frozen basil, garlic, oil

- Oil, paprika, garlic

- Lemon juice, olive oil, salt, and black pepper

- Oil and lemon pepper seasoning

- Lemon juice, cumin, oregano, sugar, salt, and black pepper

- Honey, mustard, and soy sauce

- Mustard, parsley flakes, oil, and sliced onions.

GOES WITH

158 | Grilled Flatbread

CREAMY THAI CHICKEN THIGHS

This recipe is courtesy of Chef Ami Bonen. If you enjoy going out to eat and love tasting foods from different cultures, here is a perfect, easy recipe to start with. It's creamy and has the full flavors you'd experience eating at a fusion restaurant while wondering what made the chicken taste so good.

YIELD 4-5 SERVINGS

1½-2 LB	**BONELESS SKINLESS CHICKEN THIGHS**
2 TBSP	**OIL,** FOR SAUTÉING

MARINADE

1	**SMALL ONION,** CUT INTO CHUNKS
3 TBSP	**CHOPPED PARSLEY**
1 CLOVE	**GARLIC,** PEELED AND CRUSHED
¼ TSP	**DRIED OREGANO**
1	**LEMON,** CUT INTO CHUNKS
2 TBSP	**OIL**

1 To prepare marinade, combine onion, parsley, garlic, oregano, lemon, and oil in a bowl or ziptop bag. Add the chicken and marinate in the refrigerator 6-8 hours or overnight.

2 To prepare the sauce, combine the coconut milk, peanut butter, honey, soy sauce, cilantro, garlic, and seasonings in a small saucepan over medium-high heat. Bring to a boil. Lower heat and simmer 5-8 minutes.

3 Add oil to a sauté pan over medium heat. Pan fry chicken in batches, 3-4 minutes per side. Return all chicken to pan. Add sauce. Lower heat and cook chicken and sauce together for 5-10 minutes.

SAUCE

1 14OZ CAN	**COCONUT MILK** (NOT CREAM OF COCONUT)
2 TBSP	**CREAMY PEANUT BUTTER**
1½ TBSP	**HONEY**
4 TBSP	**SOY SAUCE**
1 BUNCH	**FRESH CILANTRO,** FINELY CHOPPED
2-3 CLOVES	**GARLIC,** PEELED AND CRUSHED
¾ TSP	**SALT**
¼ TSP	**BLACK PEPPER**
⅓-½ TSP	**CURRY POWDER**
⅛ TSP	**CHILI POWDER**
⅛ TSP	**PAPRIKA**

PASTRAMI KISHKA CAPONS

YIELD 6-8 SERVINGS

6-8	**CHICKEN CAPONS** (DEBONED CHICKEN BOTTOMS)
2 TBSP	**LEMON JUICE**
•	**SALT AND PEPPER,** TO TASTE
½ TSP	**PAPRIKA**
⅔-¾ CUP	**DUCK SAUCE**

KISHKA FILLING

1½ CUPS	**FLOUR**
¼-½ CUP	**OIL**
¼ CUP	**SUGAR**
1 TSP	**SALT**
1 TBSP	**PAPRIKA**
¼-½ TSP	**BLACK PEPPER**
¾ CUP	**BOILING WATER**
4 SLICES	**PASTRAMI,** CHOPPED

1 Preheat oven to 350°F.

2 Wash the capons well. Combine lemon juice, salt, pepper, and paprika to form a rub and spread over chicken. Set aside.

3 To prepare filling, combine the flour, oil, sugar, salt, paprika, and pepper. Add the boiling water and mix well. Add the pastrami and mix until it is evenly distributed. Set aside.

4 Place one capon on a work surface, skin side down. Spoon 1½ Tablespoons of the filling onto the middle of the capon. Tuck in both ends and place the capon skin side up in a baking pan. Secure with toothpicks. Repeat with the remaining capons. Pour duck sauce over all the capons. Bake for 1½ hours or until golden brown.

APRICOT CHICKEN

This chicken needs to sit in lots of sauce while cooking, so keep the pieces tightly packed together in the pan.

1 Preheat oven to 350°F.

2 Wash and dry chicken. Rub chicken quarters with paprika, garlic, and black pepper and place into baking pan.

3 In a small bowl, combine honey, jam, onion soup mix, ketchup, and wine. Pour over chicken.

4 Cover well and bake for 2½-3 hours. Uncover during the last half hour.

YIELD 4 SERVINGS

1	**CHICKEN, CUT INTO QUARTERS**
1 TSP	**PAPRIKA**
1 CLOVE	**GARLIC,** PEELED AND CRUSHED
•	**COARSELY GROUND BLACK PEPPER,** TO TASTE
4 TBSP	**HONEY**
4 TBSP	**APRICOT JAM**
2 TBSP	**ONION SOUP MIX**
4 TBSP	**KETCHUP**
3 TBSP	**RED WINE**

ROTISSERIE-STYLE CHICKEN SKEWERS

YIELD 4-6 SERVINGS

2 TBSP	**BARBECUE SAUCE**
1 TBSP	**TERIYAKI SAUCE**
1 TBSP	**KETCHUP**
2 TBSP	**MAYONNAISE**
½ TSP	**GARLIC POWDER**
1–2 CUP	**CORNFLAKE CRUMBS**
2 LB	**CHICKEN CUTLETS,** CUT INTO STRIPS, OR 12 SMALL DRUMSTICKS, SKIN REMOVED
•	**NONSTICK COOKING SPRAY**

This is a great technique to achieve that crispy rotisserie texture and avoid sogginess. After threading the chicken on the skewers, position them over a 9x13-inch pan. The chicken will be suspended over the pan and won't need to be turned over while baking. The recipe is also delicious using drumsticks as a crunchy and tasty alternative to fried chicken.

1 Preheat oven to 350°F.

2 In a small bowl, combine BBQ sauce, teriyaki sauce, ketchup, mayonnaise, and garlic powder.

3 Pour cornflake crumbs into a shallow bowl. Dip the cutlets or drumsticks into the sauce and then coat with cornflake crumbs.

4 To cook cutlets, thread breaded strips onto wooden skewers. Spray all sides of the chicken with nonstick spray. Place skewers on a 9x13-inch pan so chicken is suspended. Bake for 25 minutes.

5 To cook drumsticks, coat the bottom of a small baking dish with cooking spray. Place drumsticks into pan. Spray with additional cooking spray. Bake, uncovered, for 1 hour and 15 minutes.

GOES WITH

44 | Mediterranean
Tomato Salad

90 | Orange-Glazed
Root Vegetables

110 | Rice Vermicelli With
Roasted Veggies

CRISPY OVEN-BAKED CHICKEN

YIELD 4 SERVINGS

EGG COATING

1	EGG
1 TBSP	MAYONNAISE

CRISPY COATING

½ CUP	FLOUR
¼ CUP	CORNMEAL
¼ CUP	CORNFLAKE CRUMBS
2 TBSP	CORNSTARCH
½ TSP	BLACK PEPPER
1 TSP	PARSLEY FLAKES
1 TSP	PAPRIKA
1 TSP	SALT
1 TSP	SUGAR
1 TSP	GARLIC POWDER

1	CHICKEN, CUT INTO EIGHTHS, OR 4 CHICKEN LEGS, EACH CUT IN HALF
2 TBSP	OIL
•	NONSTICK COOKING SPRAY

When I ask anyone what they think is their easiest chicken dish, they always answer that it's something they bread or pour sauce over and stick in the oven. Often, I prepare chicken in a pan in the morning. An hour or so before supper, I spray the top of the chicken with nonstick cooking spray and place it in the oven. The chicken comes out crispy and tasty and is always eaten up.

I use chicken with the skin on, which imparts great flavor. You can also strip the skin or use chicken cutlets cut into narrow strips in place of chicken parts.

1 Preheat oven to 350°F

2 In a shallow bowl, combine ingredients for egg coating; mix well. Using a second bowl, thoroughly combine ingredients for crispy coating.

3 Spread oil over the bottom of a 9x13-inch pan; set aside.

4 Dip chicken parts into egg mixture and then roll in crispy coating, coating well. Place in oiled pan.

5 Spray tops of chicken with cooking spray. Bake, uncovered, for 75-90 minutes.

GOES WITH

104 | Sweet Potato Fries or Garlic Fries

40 | Mrs. Weiss's Eggplant Salad

PLUM ASIAN CHICKEN

YIELD 4 SERVINGS

¼ CUP	**FLOUR**
¼ TSP	**PAPRIKA**
⅛ TSP	**BLACK PEPPER**
¼ TSP	**GARLIC**
PINCH	**SALT**
1	**CHICKEN,** CUT INTO EIGHTHS

SAUCE

2	**RIPE PLUMS,** OR NECTARINES OR PEACHES, DICED
8OZ	**TOMATO SAUCE**
1 CUP	**BROWN SUGAR**
½ CUP	**SOY SAUCE**
JUICE	**1 LEMON,** ABOUT 3 TBSP
6 TBSP	**BROWN RICE VINEGAR,** OR SAKE OR GIN

1 Preheat oven to 350°F.

2 Place all sauce ingredients into a pot over medium heat. Bring to a simmer and cook 15 minutes.

3 Combine the flour and spices. Dredge the chicken in the seasoned flour. Place into a 9x13-inch pan.

4 Pour sauce over the chicken. Cover and bake 2 hours.

NOTE

The original recipe calls for sake. If you don't have sake, you can use gin. If you don't have gin, you can use brown rice vinegar. They are not perfect replacements but they do the job.

GOES WITH

94 | Butternut Squash With Grapes and Shallots

PESTO PASTA WITH CHICKEN

YIELD 4-6 SERVINGS

½ TSP	**OREGANO**
¼ TSP	**SALT**
DASH	**BLACK PEPPER**
2 TBSP	**OIL**
¾ LB	**CHICKEN CUTLETS**
8-10	**CHERRY TOMATOES**
2-3 TBSP	**OLIVE OIL**
12 oz	**BROAD EGG NOODLES,** COOKED ACCORDING TO PACKAGE DIRECTIONS

PESTO

1 BUNCH	**BASIL LEAVES,** ABOUT 2 CUPS, 1 PACKED TIGHTLY
1½ TSP	**SALT**
2-3 CLOVES	**GARLIC**
¼ CUP	**OIL**

Traditional pesto consists of basil, garlic, and pine nuts. Since the dish has quite a bit going on, I don't find it necessary to add nuts.

1 Combine the oregano, salt, black pepper, and oil. Rub into the chicken cutlets.

2 Grill or pan fry for 6-10 minutes until cooked. Remove from pan; cut into strips, and set aside.

3 Into the same pan, add 8-10 cherry tomatoes, cut in half. Drizzle with olive oil, cook, stirring occasionally, 3-4 minutes.

4 To prepare the pesto, combine the basil, salt, and garlic in a food processor or blender. Gradually add in the oil.

5 Toss drained noodles with pesto and chicken. Top with sautéed tomatoes.

GOES WITH

30 | Roasted Tomato
Soup

CHICKEN FAJITAS

5 TBSP	**LEMON JUICE**
½ TSP	**CRUSHED RED PEPPER** (OR MORE TO TASTE)
¾ TSP	**CUMIN**
¾ TSP	**GARLIC POWDER**
1 TSP	**OREGANO**
2 TSP	**SUGAR**
½ TSP	**SALT**
1½ LBS	**CHICKEN CUTLETS,** CUT INTO THIN STRIPS
1 TBSP	**OIL**
1	**RED BELL PEPPER,** CUT INTO THIN STRIPS

WRAPS

6	**LAFFA** OR **PITA BREADS** **(9-INCH)**
1 TBSP	**OIL**
•	**GUACAMOLE** (P. 50)
•	**LETTUCE**

Chicken fajitas are a staple of Mexican cuisine, typically served in a soft tortilla. I prefer laffa bread, which is more filling, or pita, which makes it easier to eat.

This spice combination is also great to rub on chicken before it goes on the grill.

1 In a small bowl, combine the lemon juice and spices. Toss the chicken strips in the lemon-spice mixture until they are evenly coated. Allow to marinate for a minimum of 30 minutes (you can freeze the chicken strips at this point).

2 Heat the oil in a large frying pan. Add the chicken strips and cook for 5-8 minutes, until they are cooked through. Remove chicken and set aside.

3 In the same pan, sauté red pepper until slightly soft. Set aside.

4 To assemble the sandwich, warm the laffa or pita. Spread with guacamole. Top with lettuce, peppers, and chicken fajitas. Fold the bottom third of the laffa up to cover some of the filling. Then roll the entire laffa tightly from left to right. Serve with salsa and chips.

NOTE

Got leftovers? Use them in Chicken Fajitas Salad (see page 64).

GOES WITH

50 | Guacamole With Tortilla Crisps

98 | Breakfast Home Fries

BASIL CHICKEN WRAPS

YIELD 5-6 SERVINGS

3 TBSP	**OIL**
2-3	**ONIONS,** THINLY SLICED
•	**LEFTOVER CHICKEN** (3-4 CHICKEN QUARTERS)

BASIL MAYONNAISE DRESSING

4-6	**FRESH BASIL LEAVES**
½ CLOVE	**GARLIC**
½ TSP	**VINEGAR**
½ CUP	**MAYONNAISE**

5-6	**TORTILLA WRAPS**
2 CUPS	**LETTUCE,** SHREDDED

These wraps are a delicious way to make use of leftovers. You may even want to put extra chicken in your Friday night soup just so you can make this for supper during the week. Serve with a fresh salad, and no one will guess you've used your Shabbos leftovers. If you don't have wraps in the house, pita bread works well in a pinch.

1 Heat oil in a skillet over medium heat. Add onions and cook until translucent.

2 Meanwhile, remove the chicken from the bone and shred with two forks. Combine the shredded chicken with the sautéed onions and set aside.

3 To prepare the dressing, combine all ingredients. Spread the dressing on the wraps. Place lettuce over dressing. Add chicken and onions. Roll up wraps.

4 Serve at room temperature.

GOES WITH————

20 | Carrot and
Cilantro Soup

104 | Sweet-Potato
Fries

SWEET CHILI CHICKEN SANDWICH

YIELD 2 SANDWICHES

2	**CHICKEN CUTLETS,** CUT INTO STRIPS
•	**SALT AND PEPPER** TO TASTE
1 TBSP	**OIL**
1	**MEDIUM ONION,** DICED
½ CUP	**RED BELL PEPPER,** THINLY SLICED
2 TBSP	**SOY SAUCE**
2 TBSP	**THAI SWEET CHILI SAUCE** (SEE P. 80)
½ TBSP	**HONEY**

SANDWICH SPREAD

3 TBSP	**MAYONNAISE**
1 TBSP	**LEMON JUICE**
⅓ TSP	**GARLIC POWDER**
2	**ITALIAN ROLLS** OR **BAGUETTES,** SLICED OPEN
•	**LETTUCE**

Some are scared by the word "chili," thinking it represents an impossibly spicy dish. That's not so. This dish is actually quite kid-friendly and addictive. The sweet chili sauce can be as spicy or mild as you wish.

1 Season chicken with salt and pepper. Set aside.

2 Heat oil in a sauté pan over medium heat. Add onion and cook for 2 minutes. Add chicken and pepper and cook for 6 minutes, stirring constantly.

3 Add soy sauce, Thai Sweet Chili Sauce, and honey. Stir and cook an additional 2-3 minutes or until chicken is thoroughly cooked.

4 To prepare spread, combine mayonnaise, lemon juice and garlic powder. Spread over inner surface of each roll. Add lettuce. Top with chicken mixture and serve.

GOES WITH

100 | Spicy Fries

CHICKEN PANINI

YIELD 1 SANDWICH

10-INCH	**SOFT CLUB ROLL** (OR SOFT BAGUETTE)
2	**GRILLED CHICKEN CUTLETS,** SLICED
2 TBSP	**MAYONNAISE**
•	**GRILLED VEGETABLES** (SEE NOTE ON FACING PAGE)
1-2 TSP	**HONEY**
1-2 TSP	**MUSTARD**
1-2 TSP	**TERIYAKI SAUCE**
•	**OIL** OR **MARGARINE** (MELTED), FOR BRUSHING

I used to hate grilling indoors. I owned a nice big George Foreman Grill. The first time I used it, I made chicken cutlets. As hard as I tried, they were rubbery (unless eaten right away) and lacking the juicy summer grilling texture that I craved. And I really did not enjoy cleaning the grill afterward. I did try using parchment paper on the grill, which solved the cleaning difficulties — but the chicken had even less flavor.

How did I end up making use of my lovely George Foreman Grill? I make paninis, of course!

The amounts and types of dressing I use varies, depending on what I have in my refrigerator. Aside from the ingredients listed here, I've also made this recipe with Thai Sweet Chili Sauce (page 80) or spicy duck sauce. You can also cut up the chicken and mix with turkey, pastrami, or breaded chicken cutlets.

As long as you don't forget two basic rules your sandwich will come out delicious, with a juicy interior and crispy exterior:

- Use plenty of sauces/mayonnaise
- Lightly brush the outside of the sandwich with oil or melted margarine for a crispy crust.

NOTE

To grill vegetables: Place one or a combination of vegetables (zucchini, mushrooms, red or orange peppers, onion, and/or eggplant) onto a hot grill pan or panini press. Sprinkle with salt and black pepper. Drizzle with 1-2 Tablespoons oil. Grill in a grill pan or panini press until lightly browned.

To grill chicken: Rub the chicken cutlets with desired spices (salt, pepper, paprika, onion powder, garlic, cayenne, rosemary, and/or oregano) mixed with 1-2 teaspoons oil. Grill on both sides in a grill pan or in a panini press until white and center is no longer pink.

1 Slice open the roll. Spread mayonnaise on both inner surfaces of the roll. Fill with chicken and vegetables.

2 Combine the honey, mustard, and teriyaki sauce and pour over sandwich contents. Close the sandwich.

3 Brush both outer sides of the bread with oil or margarine.

4 Preheat panini grill or grill pan.

5 To cook, place the sandwich on the hot pan. Close lid on panini grill, or if using a grill pan, press the sandwich down well, using a heavy pot.

6 Turn sandwich over and press down again to attain grill marks on both sides.

BEER BEEF STEW

2 LB	**BEEF STEW MEAT**
•	**SALT, BLACK PEPPER, PAPRIKA,** TO TASTE
2 TBSP	**OIL**
2-3	**LARGE ONIONS,** CUT INTO WEDGES
1½ CUPS (12oz)	**LIGHT BEER**
1	**BAY LEAF**
2 TBSP	**BROWN SUGAR**
2 TBSP	**VINEGAR**

For tough meat, beer is a wonderful tenderizer. For batters, it acts as a mild leavening agent, causing your crust to puff up.

Now — here's a little secret why I believe the simplest recipes are usually the best. It's not the number of ingredients and complicated steps that make a dish delicious. If the flavor combination is right, the food will really pop. Beer and onion is one of those combinations that work in harmony. Think tomato and basil, honey and mustard, garlic and parsley — beer and onion belongs right there on that list. Since beer has a slightly bitter yet sweet taste, caramelized onion makes for a perfect match.

1 Season meat with salt, black pepper, and paprika. Heat the oil in a large sauté pan over high heat. Sear meat on all sides (you may need to do it in 2 batches). Remove meat and set aside.

2 Add onion wedges to pan and sauté for 10-12 minutes. Add beef, beer, bay leaf, brown sugar, and vinegar. Adjust heat to low. Cook, covered, for 1½ hours. Continue cooking for an additional 30 minutes, with the cover slightly open. Then raise heat and cook, uncovered, for 10-15 minutes or until the sauce is reduced.

3 Remove bay leaf before serving.

GOES WITH_____

86 | Onion Blossoms

SHREDDED BEEF

YIELD 8 SERVINGS

2 LB	**CHUCK** OR **OTHER ROAST**
¼ CUP	**BROWN SUGAR**
1	**ONION,** SLICED
2 TBSP	**ONION SOUP MIX**
5 CLOVES	**GARLIC,** PEELED
¾ CUP	**KETCHUP**
½ CUP	**LIGHT BEER**
8	**BUNS** OR **CLUB ROLLS,** OPTIONAL

Tough meat such as chuck is the perfect candidate for beer. The beer tenderizes the meat, and the long cooking in a slow cooker results in succulent meat that falls apart. This is a real kid pleaser, even though half the kids I know forgo the bun and eat the meat plain.

1 Place meat into the slow cooker. Sprinkle the meat with brown sugar, onion slices, onion soup mix and garlic cloves. Pour the ketchup and the beer over the meat. Cover and cook on low for 8-10 hours or on high for 5 hours.

2 Remove the meat. Strain the liquid from the slow cooker; discard solids. Reserve liquid. Set aside the juices from the slow cooker. With two forks, shred meat, discarding any large pieces of fat. Place shredded meat back into the pot and pour about half the strained liquid over it. Cover the pot and cook on high for 20-30 minutes.

3 Serve in buns or club rolls with desired toppings, if desired.

NOTE

The more beer is cooked and reduced, the stronger its flavor will be. If the dish requires long cooking and reduction, avoid using too strong a brew. Go with a light beer as suggested.

GOES WITH

98 | Breakfast Home Fries

CHIMICHURRI SKEWERED STEAKS

YIELD 6 SERVINGS

CHIMICHURRI SAUCE

1 BUNCH	**PARSLEY**
7 CLOVES	**GARLIC**
¼ CUP	**VINEGAR**
1 TBSP	**LEMON JUICE**
½ TSP	**SALT**
½ TSP	**BLACK PEPPER**
¾ CUP	**OLIVE OIL**
12 PORTIONS	**SANDWICH STEAK**
12	**WOODEN SKEWERS,** SOAKED IN WATER FOR 30 MINUTES

Sandwich steaks are thinly sliced shoulder steaks.

1   To prepare the sauce, use a food processor or blender to combine the parsley, garlic, vinegar, lemon juice, salt, and pepper. Slowly drizzle in the oil; process until combined. Divide sauce. Combine meat with half the sauce and marinate in the refrigerator for 4-6 hours. Reserve remaining sauce for serving.

2   Thread steaks onto soaked skewers and arrange on a baking sheet.

3   Position rack in the center of the oven. Broil steaks, 5-8 minutes on each side, or until desired doneness.

4   Serve each skewer with a little reserved chimichurri sauce.

NOTE

Chimichurri is an Argentinean green sauce or marinade made from parsley, garlic, oil, vinegar, and sometimes red pepper flakes. You can toss it with roasted potatoes, spread on sandwiches, or use as a dip. It's a wonderful marinade for chicken, beef, or fish. Skirt steak and sandwich steaks make an especially great match, as in this recipe!

GOES WITH

108 | Mexican Rice

ASIAN BURGERS

1 LB	**GROUND BEEF**
3-4 TBSP	**SOY SAUCE**
1½ TBSP	**SUGAR**
2 CLOVES	**GARLIC,** PEELED AND CRUSHED
1 TBSP	**OIL**
1 TBSP	**SESAME SEEDS**
3 TBSP	**DICED SCALLIONS,** WHITE AND LIGHT GREEN PARTS ONLY
•	**PINCH BLACK PEPPER**
4	**HAMBURGER BUNS** (OR 8 SMALLER BUNS), OPTIONAL

I love to make these small, just because they are so cute and perfect for little fingers.

1 Combine all ingredients and form into 4 large or 8 small patties.

2 Fry, grill or broil patties in oven for 5 minutes on one side and 6-8 minutes on the second side. Adjust cooking time if you are making the smaller burgers.

3 Serve on buns with desired toppings (optional).

NOTE

This meat mixture freezes very well. Form into patties and freeze them raw with parchment paper between each layer.

GOES WITH

49 | Roasted Mushroom and Pepper Salad

46 | Nutty Cabbage Salad

ORANGE-GLAZED FLANKEN

YIELD 6 SERVINGS

6 STRIPS	**FLANKEN,** BONE-IN
1½ CUPS	**HOT AND SPICY DUCK SAUCE**
1 CUP	**ORANGE JUICE**
¼ TSP	**PAPRIKA**
¼ TSP	**GARLIC POWDER**

This recipe works well with flanken on the bone or with spare ribs.

• Place flanken in a 9x13-inch pan. In a small bowl, combine remaining ingredients and pour over flanken. Bake at 350°F for 2 hours covered. Uncover and bake for an additional 20-30 minutes.

GLAZED LAMB OR VEAL CHOPS

YIELD 4-6 SERVINGS

2	**MEDIUM ONIONS,** SLICED
4 TBSP	**ONION SOUP MIX,** DIVIDED
5 TBSP	**APRICOT JAM,** DIVIDED
4	**LAMB CUTLETS, 6 LAMB CHOPS** OR **4 VEAL CHOPS**

This is a gourmet dish that takes a minute to assemble.

1 Preheat oven to 350°F.

2 Layer half the onion slices in a 9x13-inch pan. Sprinkle with 2 Tablespoons onion soup mix and dot with 2 Tablespoons apricot jam. Place lamb or veal chops on top. Dot with remaining apricot jam, sprinkle with onion soup mix, and top with remaining onions.

3 Cover pan very tightly with foil. Bake for 1½ hours. Uncover and bake for an additional ½ hour.

GOES WITH

112 | Honey-Mustard
Couscous

88 | Caramelized
Shallots

BEEF WITH CARAMELIZED PEARL ONIONS

This dish is best served re-warmed. As long as there are ample juices, the longer you cook it, the more succulent it will be.

YIELD 8 SERVINGS

3 LBS	**BEEF STEW MEAT**
2 TBSP	**OIL**
1	**LARGE CARROT,** THINLY SLICED
1	**LARGE ONION,** DICED
1 TSP	**SALT**
¼ TSP	**PEPPER**
2 TBSP	**FLOUR**
2 CUPS	**RED WINE**
3 CUPS	**CHICKEN STOCK**
2 CLOVES	**GARLIC,** PEELED
18-24	**PEARL ONIONS**

1. Rinse meat and pat dry with a paper towel. Heat oil in a sauté pan and brown meat on all sides. Remove and set aside.

2. Add carrot and onion to the pan and cook until onions are soft. Return meat to pan. Season with salt and pepper. Stir in the flour and mix well. Add wine, stock, and garlic. Bring to a simmer.

3. Cook, covered, for 1 hour. Uncover and cook for an additional ½ hour.

4. Place pearl onions into a bowl. Pour boiling water over the onions and let rest for 3 minutes. Drain water from the onions and peel away outer layer.

5. Add onions to the meat and continue cooking for an additional 45 minutes to 1 hour.

NOTE

Beef stew is cut up pieces of mock tender meat (sometimes called shoulder kolichal). You can also use chuck cut into small cubes.

SWEET POTATO CHIPS (PARVE)

Select long and narrow sweet potatoes. Using a vegetable peeler, cut very thin round slices from each sweet potato. Deep fry until chips turn a golden orange. (Keep a close eye on them as the chips will be ready really quickly.) Season with salt.

GOES WITH

66 | Warm Sweet-
Potato Salad

OR

116 | Confetti Orzo

BBQ PEPPER STEAK

YIELD 4-6 SERVINGS

3 TBSP	**OIL**
2 LB	**PEPPER STEAK**
1 CUP	**WATER**
½ CUP	**BARBECUE SAUCE**
4 CLOVES	**GARLIC,** PEELED AND CRUSHED
2 TBSP	**SOY SAUCE**
¼ CUP	**KETCHUP**
1 TBSP	**LEMON JUICE**
2 TBSP	**BROWN SUGAR**
½ TBSP	**PAPRIKA**
½ TSP	**SALT**
DASH	**BLACK PEPPER**

Most pepper steak recipes call for vegetables and oriental flavors. Well, my brothers don't like vegetables with their pepper steak, so this is a version for them and for other picky eaters who just want the meat. This recipe is much saucier than traditional pepper steak, so the meat will remain soft.

1 Heat the oil in a large sauté pan over medium-high heat. Add pepper steak and cook on all sides until lightly browned.

2 In a small bowl, combine remaining ingredients and pour over steak. Lower the heat, cover, and cook for 1½ hours. Uncover and simmer for an additional ½ hour.

CARAMELIZED FRENCH ROAST

YIELD 10-12 SERVINGS

3 TO 4 LB	**FRENCH ROAST**
•	**SALT AND PEPPER,** TO TASTE
•	**PAPRIKA,** TO TASTE
1⅓ CUP	**SUGAR**
2	**LARGE ONIONS,** SLICED INTO ROUNDS
2 TBSP	**FLOUR**
2 TBSP	**COLD WATER**

When my friend Krassie shared this recipe with me, I started dreaming about how delicious it is before I even tasted it.

1 Rinse the French roast and pat dry. Season well with salt, pepper, and paprika. Place the sugar in a sauté pan (it should also be large enough to fit the meat, covered). Over low heat, cook sugar, stirring occasionally, until sugar melts and turns caramel in color. Add the meat to the pan. Using a fork or tongs, rotate the meat, searing on each side two times.

2 When all surfaces of the meat are browned, lift the roast and place the onions underneath. As the onions cook, they will release juice that will mix with the sugar, creating a sauce. Cover and let cook over medium low heat for 3 hours. (Make sure the heat is low enough not to burn the meat, but high enough so that the sauce is still simmering slightly.) Remove meat from pan.

3 In a small bowl, combine the flour and water. Add to the sauce. Cook until the sauce thickens. Slice meat and serve with caramelized onion sauce.

NOTE

To freeze and rewarm, slightly undercook the roast. Freeze the meat and sugar-onion sauce separately. Rewarm the sauce, only adding the flour and water at this point. Slice the meat and reheat with the sauce.

COOKING WITH WINE

If you don't want to use sugar, try my version of this roast cooked in wine. Season the meat with paprika and fresh garlic. Rub meat with 1 Tablespoon canola oil. Heat 2-3 Tablespoons oil in a sauté pan over medium heat. Sear the meat on all sides. Remove meat from pot. Add two diced onions to the sauté pan and cook 10 minutes, or until soft. Return the meat and a full (750 liter) bottle of dry red wine to the pot. Cover and cook 3 hours. Transfer meat to a platter or cutting board; let cool. Slice, return slices to sauce in pan, and rewarm in the oven.

FLANKEN EGG ROLLS

YIELD 16-18 EGG ROLLS

2 LB	**FLANKEN**
4-5	**LARGE ONIONS, SLICED**
•	**SALT AND BLACK PEPPER,** TO TASTE
1¼ TSP	**GARLIC POWDER**
4 TBSP	**TERIYAKI SAUCE**
2 CLOVES	**GARLIC,** PEELED AND CRUSHED
16-18	**EGG ROLL** OR **SPRING ROLL WRAPPERS**

This is a man's egg roll — without vegetables. The meat that works best in this recipe is boneless flanken. It's expensive, but it has very little fat. You can use a cheaper meat, but you'll need to cut away the fat.

1 Place flanken onto the onions in a large pot. Season with salt, black pepper, and garlic powder. Cook over low heat for 2-3 hours.

2 Remove from heat and shred meat. Add the teriyaki sauce to the meat/onion mixture. Add crushed garlic.

3 To roll, position egg roll wrapper in a diamond shape. Brush all the edges with water. Place a spoonful of filling onto the lower third of the wrapper. Fold the bottom corner over the filling. Fold in the right and left sides toward the center. Continue rolling until the top corner folds over, pressing to seal.

4 Heat oil in a deep fryer at 325°F or in a pot over medium heat. Fry for 4 minutes.

5 Drain on paper towels and serve hot.

6 Serve with duck sauce or Thai Sweet Chili Sauce (see page 80) as a dipping sauce.

CITRUS SEA BASS

YIELD 6-8 SERVINGS

6 SLICES	**SEA BASS**
½ CUP	**LEMON JUICE**
PINCH	**SALT AND PEPPER**

GLAZE

2 CUPS	**ORANGE JUICE**
1 CUP	**APRICOT JAM**
1 TBSP	**ONION SOUP MIX**

1 Preheat oven to 350°F.

2 In a bowl or ziptop bag, marinate sea bass in lemon juice, salt and pepper for 1 hour in the refrigerator. Transfer fish to baking dish. Discard marinade.

3 Bake, uncovered, for 20 minutes.

4 Meanwhile, prepare the glaze. In a small saucepan over medium heat, combine orange juice, jam, and onion soup mix. Cook for an additional 15 minutes, stirring occasionally until slightly thickened.

5 Pour glaze over sea bass. Bake an additional 10-15 minutes.

TERIYAKI SALMON SKEWERS

I find that salmon is one of those things that we tend to serve the same way over and over again ... and quickly get tired of it. This recipe comes from my sister-in-law, and it's currently one of the most popular ones I make. For a weekday meal, you can skip the skewers and vegetables and pour the sauce over fillets of salmon.

YIELD 4-6 SERVINGS

2 TBSP	**TERIYAKI SAUCE**
2 TBSP	**BROWN SUGAR**
2 TBSP	**KETCHUP**
4 SLICES	**SALMON FILLET,** SKIN REMOVED, EACH CUT INTO 4-6 CUBES
•	**WOODEN SKEWERS**
•	**SESAME SEEDS,** OPTIONAL, FOR GARNISH

RECOMMENDED VEGETABLES

- **CHERRY TOMATOES**
- **RED BELL PEPPER**
- **SMALL BUTTON MUSHROOMS**
- **PEARL ONION**

1 Preheat the oven to 350°F.

2 Combine the teriyaki sauce, brown sugar, and ketchup in a shallow bowl or ziptop bag. Marinate salmon cubes in the mixture for 30 minutes in the refrigerator.

3 Thread the salmon cubes and vegetables onto skewers. Discard marinade. Bake, uncovered, for 20 minutes.

4 Garnish with sesame seeds, if desired.

SUNDRIED TOMATO SALMON

PARVE

This recipe is from my mother's personal cookbook; it would often grace her table on special occasions. It's not too complicated, but very different from the typical ways salmon is served. You don't have to serve it on skewers — that's just an elegant touch. For a less fussy meal, keep the skin on the whole fillets and simply pour on the sauce before baking.

1 Preheat oven to 350°F.

2 Combine sundried tomatoes with olive oil, garlic, salt, and pepper in a shallow bowl or ziptop bag. Marinate salmon in sundried tomato mixture for 20 minutes.

3 Thread salmon onto skewers. Discard marinade. Place skewers into a baking dish lined with parchment paper. Bake, uncovered, for 20-30 minutes.

YIELD 4 SERVINGS

5-6 PIECES	**SUNDRIED TOMATOES,** CHOPPED
3 TBSP	**OLIVE OIL**
2-3 CLOVES	**GARLIC,** PEELED AND CRUSHED
•	**SALT AND PEPPER** TO TASTE
3	**SALMON FILLETS,** SKIN REMOVED, CUT INTO NUGGETS OR STRIPS
4	**WOODEN SKEWERS**

SALMON WITH PINE NUTS & CREAM SAUCE

YIELD 4 SERVINGS

½ CUP	**BREADCRUMBS**
½ CUP	**PINE NUTS**
4	**SALMON FILLETS**
2 TBSP	**MUSTARD**

CREAM SAUCE

2 TBSP	**LEMON JUICE**
¼ CUP	**HEAVY CREAM**
¼ CUP	**BUTTER**
⅛ TSP	**SALT**
⅛ TSP	**BLACK PEPPER**

This is a very quick salmon recipe that is best served fresh.

1 Preheat oven to 350°F.

2 Spread breadcrumbs on a baking sheet and toast for 10 minutes at 350°F. Add the pine nuts and set aside.

3 Rinse the salmon in cold water and place in a pan. Spread mustard over the salmon and pack the breadcrumb mixture on top.

4 Bake, uncovered, for 15-20 minutes.

5 While fish is baking, prepare the cream sauce. Place the lemon juice into a small saucepan. Over low heat, reduce the lemon juice to 1 Tablespoon. Add the heavy cream. Bring to a boil.

6 Reduce heat and allow to cook for 3 additional minutes. Add the butter and whisk until it melts. Season with salt and pepper. Serve over fillets.

GOES WITH

52 | Parmesan
Citrus Salad

PISTACHIO-CRUSTED TILAPIA

PARVE

YIELD 4 SERVINGS

¾ CUP	**SHELLED PISTACHIOS**
2 CLOVES	**GARLIC,** PEELED AND CRUSHED
•	**SALT AND PEPPER,** TO TASTE
½ CUP	**OLIVE OIL**
3 TBSP	**YELLOW MUSTARD**
4	**TILAPIA FILLETS**

R. Horowitz was sitting in the doctor's office, reading a magazine. She was reading a recipe for tilapia when she was called in for her appointment. When she got home, she couldn't remember the exact ingredients or directions, but we think it might have been something like this.

1 Preheat oven to 350°F.

2 Using a food processor, combine pistachios, garlic, salt,* and pepper. With the motor running, slowly drizzle in the olive oil to form a paste.

3 Spread mustard over surface of fish and pack the pistachio paste on top, forming a crust.

4 Bake, uncovered, for 20 minutes. Serve over linguini.

*If you use salted pistachios, you may not need salt.

GOES WITH

26 | Cream of
Leek Soup

DILL SALMON

Some recipes are acquired through marriage, when the culinary secrets of another family become ours as well. This is credited to my sister-in-law's mother.

YIELD 6 SERVINGS

6	**SALMON FILLETS**
1 HEAPING TSP	**MUSTARD**
½ CUP	**OLIVE OIL**
5 CLOVES	**GARLIC,** PEELED AND CRUSHED
½ CUP	**FRESH DILL,** CHOPPED
1 TSP	**ONION SOUP MIX**

1 Preheat oven to 350°F.

2 Line a baking pan with parchment paper. Place fish in pan.

3 In a small bowl, thoroughly combine mustard, olive oil, garlic, dill, and onion soup mix. Dividing mixture evenly, coat fillets.

4 Bake, covered, for 25 minutes.

GOES WITH

114 | Couscous with Vegetables

TRADITIONAL FOODS

Week after week, the same traditional foods appear on my table. Although I do like to try new recipes, my family expects the same Ashkenaz dishes every Shabbos and Yom Tov.

It may not be a *law*, but there *are* reasons for our traditional foods. The Talmud says that those who honor the Shabbos with three meals are greatly rewarded and spared from suffering.

The prophet Isaiah says, "If you proclaim the Shabbos a delight ...," the reward will be the heritage of our forefather Jacob. The Gemara tells us that the "delight" of Shabbos is its special food, including a big fish. That is why we eat fish on Shabbos. Many people eat fish at all three meals.

Jews are taught to find ways to serve Hashem even when we eat and to find lessons about holy things even in "ordinary" recipes. That is why we eat traditional Shabbos foods. Here are a few lessons that our teachers found in food.

Shabbos foods remind us of the manna that our ancestors ate in the desert. Does *kugel* remind you of the manna? The Rama says that *kugel* has a crust on the top and on the bottom to remind us of the manna that was coated with dew both on top and underneath. The Rebbe of Apta cites the Midrash that the manna had almost any taste, except that of fish or onions. We eat fish and have onions with our egg salad on Shabbos to experience *every* flavor on this special day.

The Hebrew word for fish is *dag*, spelled *daled gimel*, with the numerical value of 7 — a reminder that fish is a specialty in honor of Shabbos, the seventh day.

The *Matteh Moshe* tells us that when Mashiach comes, Hashem will honor us with a banquet, serving the *Leviasan*, a giant fish. On Shabbos, when you enjoy your delicious gefilte fish or salmon, think about Mashiach and the mouthwatering taste of the *Leviasan*.

The *Shulchan Aruch* reminds us that the Torah permits us to use fire on Shabbos and to prepare cooked food for the holy day — but we have to use the fire properly. That's why we prepare cholent on Friday and let it simmer all night, to be enjoyed at our daytime Shabbos *seudah*.

Even the thin soup noodles have special meaning. They intertwine, symbolizing unity. Hashem wants us to always help one another and show concern for our fellow Jews.

This is just a small sample of the many wonderful things about our traditional foods. Isn't it great that we can be rewarded for eating scrumptious foods? Enjoy your Shabbos meal!

TRADITIONAL

FOUR-SECTION CHALLAH ROLLS

- **ONE BATCH OF CHALLAH DOUGH** (USE YOUR FAVORITE RECIPE)

- **EGG WASH**

4 **TOPPINGS OF YOUR CHOICE** (ONION FLAKES, SESAME SEEDS, POPPY SEEDS, SUNFLOWER SEEDS, DRIED ROSEMARY)

Use your own challah recipe to assemble these rolls. They are a bit time consuming but result in a beautiful presentation that's perfect for a *seudah*, *sheva brachos*, or any party.

1 Form balls of dough. For perfectly sized balls, I recommend weighing each piece of dough at 3.5 oz. Pull all corners to one central point, while forming a ball on the reverse side. Pinch ends together and place seam side down on a baking sheet lined with parchment paper.

2 Roll another piece of dough into a thin rope, 5 inches long. Cut the rope into 2 separate strands. Position the 2 strands over the ball to form an "x" shape. This will divide the roll into four sections. Tuck the end of the strands under the roll.

3 Repeat until all dough is used up or desired number of rolls are formed. Place rolls on prepared baking sheet and cover with towel.

4 Preheat oven to 350°F.

5 Let rise 15 minutes and brush tops of rolls with beaten egg wash. Use a different topping to garnish each of the four sections.

6 Bake for 20 minutes or until golden brown. When you tap the bottom of the roll, it should sound hollow.

EGG WASH 411

Egg yolk + water =
A shiny golden amber color

Whole egg + water =
Golden yellowish-brown surface

Whole egg + salt =
Shiny finish

Egg white + water =
A crispy lighter color crust

Egg white + salt =
A lighter crust

Using sugar instead of salt results in a slightly sweeter crust.

EGG & LIVER TOWER

1 8oz CAN	**EMPTIED OF ALL CONTENTS**
•	**OIL,** TO BRUSH CAN
•	**PREPARED EGG SALAD**
•	**PREPARED CHOPPED LIVER SALAD**
1	**LARGE TOMATO,** SLICED INTO THIN ROUNDS

CRISPY ONIONS

1 CUP	**OIL**
1	**LARGE ONION,** THINLY SLICED INTO ROUNDS

Adding height in food presentation makes everything look better, and you can achieve this without going out to buy another kitchen gadget (I refuse to!). This isn't so much a recipe as it is a suggestion for presentation. Everyone has a preferred egg salad and/or chopped liver recipe, or knows where to buy the family's favorite. Have fun plating these towers and your table will be simply elegant — and no one has to know how easy they were to assemble!

Try these towers with potatoes and/or sweet potatoes.

The crispy onions on top used to be something my husband would buy before every Shabbos. He said, "There has to be something you can't make." Oh yeah? (For instructions, see note on facing page.)

1 Using a can opener, remove both ends of the can, forming a ring mold. Wash thoroughly. Brush the inside of the can with oil and set in the center of your serving plate. Add 3-4 Tablespoons liver. Pat down well.

2 Position a slice of tomato over the liver; it should cover entirely. Add 3-4 heaping Tablespoons egg salad. Pat down well.

3 Carefully remove the ring mold and garnish with crispy onions.

4 Repeat with remaining liver, tomato, egg salad, and onions.

Make sure your egg salad has enough oil or mayonnaise to hold it together. Dry egg salad will not maintain the shape of the mold.

CRISPY ONIONS

These onions make for a stunning topping. Use over mashed potatoes, meats, or eat as-is when no one is watching!

Heat the oil in a small saucepan over high heat. When hot, add the onions and reduce heat to low. Simmer for 12-15 minutes, stirring them with a fork every so often, until they turn a golden brown (it may take longer depending on your pan).

Place paper towels on a flat tray or pan. Spread the cooked onions in a single layer over the paper towels and let dry. The onions will crisp up while drying.

LAZY MAN'S CHOLENT

4	**LARGE POTATOES,** SKIN ON, HALVED
3	**LARGE ONIONS,** HALVED
1 CUP	**BARLEY**
8 CLOVES	**GARLIC,** PEELED AND LEFT WHOLE
5-6 TBSP	**ONION SOUP MIX,** OR TO TASTE
16 OZ BAG	**CHOLENT BEAN MIX**
5-7 DASHES	**TABASCO SAUCE**
12 OZ BOTTLE	**CHILI SAUCE** (I LIKE HEINZ)
5-6 CUPS	**WATER**
2-3 PIECES	**FLANKEN ON THE BONE,** CUT IN HALF

Men definitely outnumber woman when it comes to making a top cholent. Recently, I received this recipe from my uncle and I couldn't get over the fact that this must be the laziest cholent ever. Can it be that you don't even peel the potatoes and all you do is dump them in the crockpot? My tasters — I served it to a group of teenage boys — gave it rave reviews. It's really easy and great for a crowd.

1 Begin the cholent preparation 24 hours before consumption. Line a slow cooker with a plastic slow-cooker liner. Layer the potatoes on the bottom. Layer onions, barley, garlic, cholent beans, Tabasco sauce, and chili sauce, in order. Do not stir. Top with the flanken.

2 Add 5-6 cups water to the slow cooker. Cook on high until cholent begins to bubble. Turn to low and cook 24 hours.

3 If you like to add potato kugel or kishka to your cholent, bury it slightly under the top level and add a small amount of additional hot water before Shabbos. Most important of all — do not stir this at any time!

NOTE

CHOLENT-MAKING TIPS

- Soak beans overnight in water
- Sear the meat in oil
- Place kugel in baking paper
- Season well
- Layer meat and beans in the crock-pot so that the meat doesn't dry out.

MORE SEASONINGS

- Brown sugar
- Ketchup
- Onion soup mix
- Honey
- Beer
- Coke
- Coffee
- Crushed red pepper

WORTH ADDING

- Kishka
- Pickled pastrami roll
- Potato kugel
- Franks
- Eggs
- Baby potatoes
- Jachnun
- Pipiklech or drumsticks

PARVE POLISH CHOLENT

YIELD 12 SERVINGS

8–10	**MEDIUM RED POTATOES**
3 TBSP	**SALT**
16 oz BAG	**MIXED CHOLENT BEANS**
½–¾ CUP	**OIL**
•	**WATER,** TO COVER

This pareve cholent comes from my sister-in-law. This recipe was passed down as a Polish cholent and it is made exactly the way it was made it in Poland. The first instructions were to peel and salt the potatoes and leave them overnight. On Friday morning, I woke up to see horrible murky black water with potatoes that looked as if they had grown moldy overnight. I was ready to toss the entire lot into the garbage and move on to my trusty version. Then curiosity got the best of me and I continued with the strange instructions. My testers thought this one was worth 10 stars. It's light, salty, and buttery.

1 Peel the potatoes and cut into large chunks. Place them into a bowl. Pour salt over the potatoes, mix, and leave them out overnight (not in water).

2 Soak the beans overnight in water to cover.

3 On Friday morning, the potatoes should have taken on a black/brown color and will have produced a liquid. Do not throw out the liquid! (This is part of the liquid used in the cholent.)

4 Pour the potatoes and their liquid into a 6-quart pot, add beans and oil, and cover with water. Cook over medium heat for a few hours.

5 An hour or so before Shabbos, place the pot on a hot plate on the lowest heat possible that allows the liquid to keep bubbling. Leave on hot plate until ready to serve.

CARAMELIZED ONION KISHKA

PARVE

The caramelized onions add a twist to the traditional parve kishka.

1 Heat the oil in a skillet over medium heat. Add onion and cook until golden brown. Set aside.

2 Combine flour, cornflake crumbs, and seasoning. Add oil to mixture. Gradually add water until the mixture is firm and soft.

3 Roll out the mixture to the size of a baking sheet. Spread with the onions. Roll up, jellyroll style, to form a thin and narrow log. Cut into 5 pieces (or desired size) and freeze until ready to serve.

4 Add one piece of frozen kishka directly into the cholent pot when liquid in pot is bubbling. Continue to cook as usual.

5 Slice into rounds when serving cholent.

YIELD 5 SEGMENTS, EACH 4 SERVINGS

3 TBSP	**OIL**
1	**LARGE ONION,** DICED
3 CUPS	**FLOUR**
1 CUP	**CORNFLAKE CRUMBS**
1¼ TBSP	**SALT**
1 TBSP	**PAPRIKA**
1 TBSP	**PEPPER,** OR TO TASTE
¾ CUP	**OIL**
1 CUP	**COLD WATER**

OVERNIGHT POTATO KUGEL

YIELD 8-10 SERVINGS

5 LB	**POTATOES,** PEELED
1	**LARGE ONION**
8	**EGGS**
1 CUP	**OIL**
½ CUP	**BOILING WATER**
1½ TBSP	**SALT**
⅛ TSP	**BLACK PEPPER**

For every hundred people who want to learn how to make a good overnight kugel, there are about a hundred different ways to make it. Some people make a regular potato kugel and pour hot water over it, cover, and bake. Some people pour a raw potato kugel mixture into the slow cooker (that's also a good way). This one is an all-around favorite.

1 Preheat oven to 350°F.

2 Grate the potatoes and onion. Mix in the eggs, oil, and boiling water. Season with salt and pepper.

3 Transfer the potato mixture to a 9x13-inch pan. Bake for 2 hours, uncovered. After 2 hours, cover tightly with 3 layers of foil. Place a 9x13-inch pan filled halfway with cold water on the bottom rack of the oven. Place the covered kugel on the oven rack directly above the water. Lower oven temperature to 220°F and bake for 8 hours or overnight.

I use a Braun food processor that has a kugel blade, and I set the speed on 8, so it isn't too stringy or too mushy. On any food processor, slower speeds will yield stringier pieces and faster speeds will yield mushier pieces, so stick to a medium speed. For years, my mother did not think that a food processor could make good potato kugel. She had her special grater — and that was the only tool that could be used! With boys in the family who were crazy about potato kugel, we had to peel and grate about 15 pounds of potatoes each week. We'd each take turns at the grater until it was all done. Nowadays, my mother agrees that the Braun does a really fine job.

SIMANIM

We eat *simanim* on the night of Rosh Hashanah as omens for a good year. The names of the foods in Hebrew and Aramaic hint at the blessings, for us to have a good year, and for the evil decree of our sentence to be torn up.

Apples and Honey
"May it be Your will, Hashem our G-d and the G-d of our forefathers, that You renew us for a good and sweet year."

Head of a fish or sheep
"May ... we be as the head and not as the tail."

Pomegranates
"May ... our merits increase like pomegranate [seeds]."

Dates
"May ... our enemies be consumed."

CARAMELIZED CARROTS

PARVE

"May ... our merits increase."

YIELD 2 CUPS

8	CARROTS
½ CUP	OIL
1 CUP	SUGAR
JUICE	ONE LEMON
DASH	SALT

1. Peel the carrots and slice thinly.

2. In a small pot, heat the oil. Add the carrots and sauté for 5 minutes.

3. Add the sugar, lemon juice, and salt.

4. Cook, covered, over low heat for 45-60 minutes. Uncover the last 5-10 minutes. Stir occasionally.

LEEK PATTIES

PARVE

"May ... our enemies be destroyed."

YIELD 20-24 PATTIES

1 Cut off the dark green part off the leeks and discard. Slice the leeks in half lengthwise and wash thoroughly. Cut the leek into strips and dice.

2 Place leeks into a pot with enough water to cover. Add 2 Tablespoons oil. Bring to a boil to eliminate raw oniony flavor. Remove from heat.

3 Drain very, very well, pressing out excess water.

4 Add the eggs, crumbs, salt, and sugar. Form the batter into patties. If the batter is very loose, add a bit more bread crumbs.

5 Pour a thin layer of oil into a skillet over medium heat and bring to frying temperature. Slip patties into hot oil and fry until browned on one side. Flip patties and brown the other side.

6 Serve cold or at room temperature.

3	**LARGE LEEKS** (OR 4 SMALLER ONES), **WHITE AND LIGHT GREEN PARTS ONLY**
●	**WATER, AS NEEDED**
2 TBSP	**OIL**
3	**EGGS**
1 TBSP	**BREADCRUMBS** OR **MATZAH MEAL**
●	**SALT**
PINCH	**SUGAR**
●	**OIL,** FOR FRYING

GOURDS

3-4	**CHAYOTE SQUASH**
•	**JUICE OF ½ LEMON**
1½ CUP	**SUGAR**
½ CUP	**WATER**
DASH	**SALT**

"May ... our merits be read before You and the [evil] decree of our sentence be torn up."

Strictly speaking, the gourd family of vegetables includes cucumbers, melons, pumpkins, and squash — the latter of which is our custom to use for this siman.

1 Cut the squash in half. Using a spoon, remove the seeds and pith. Dice, with the peel, into small cubes.

2 Place into a small pot. Add lemon juice, sugar, water, and salt.

3 Cook 1 to 1 ½ hours until caramelized and candy-like.

BLACK-EYED PEAS

½ LB	**BLACK-EYED PEAS**
•	**WATER,** FOR SOAKING AND COOKING
1 CUP	**SUGAR**
1 TBSP	**LEMON JUICE**
DASH	**SALT**

"May ... our merits increase."

1 Soak the peas overnight in water.

2 Drain peas. Place into a pot and cover with fresh water. Add sugar, lemon juice, and salt.

3 Cook, covered, until the water has cooked off and the peas are very soft, about 2 to 3 hours. You may need to add more water if peas aren't soft enough.

BEET LEAF PATTIES

"May ... our adversaries be removed."

The beet leaves shrink all the way down, so don't worry if they fill the entire pot at first. Many use spinach or Swiss chard, in this recipe.

1 Wash the beet leaves very, very well. Remove the leaves from the stalks; discard stalks.

2 Place the beet leaves into a pot. Cook over low heat until they shrink and are very soft. Stir with a fork occasionally to break up leaves.

3 Drain very, very well. Combine with eggs, breadcrumbs, salt, and sugar. Form into small patties.

4 Pour a thin layer of oil into a skillet over medium heat and bring to frying temperature. Slip patties into hot oil and fry until browned on one side. Flip patties and brown the other side.

YIELD 18 PATTIES

8 BUNCHES	**BEET LEAVES** (EACH BUNCH IS ABOUT 6 LEAVES)
3	**EGGS**
1 TBSP	**BREADCRUMBS** OR **MATZAH MEAL**
DASH	**SALT**
DASH	**SUGAR**

KREPLACH

3 CUPS	**FLOUR**
3	**EGGS**
•	**PINCH SALT**
3 TBSP	**WATER**
6 QUARTS	**WATER,** FOR COOKING

CHEESE FILLING (DAIRY)

1 LB	**FARMER CHEESE**
1	**EGG YOLK**
⅓ CUP	**SUGAR**
1 TBSP	**FARINA** OR **FLOUR**
•	**BREADCRUMBS**
•	**CONFECTIONER'S SUGAR,** FOR DUSTING

CHICKEN FILLING (MEAT)

½ LB	**CHICKEN LIVER,** BROILED
2 TBSP	**OIL**
•	**PAPRIKA, SALT, AND PEPPER,** TO TASTE
½ LB	**COOKED CHICKEN**
1	**EGG**

Three times a year, my grandmother will make and freeze hundreds of kreplach, making up for the rest of us who are too lazy to try. The chicken kreplach will be added to soup, while the dairy ones are breaded and fried. Maybe it's time to uphold tradition and make a batch ourselves.

1   To prepare dough, in a mixer fitted with the dough hook, mix dough ingredients until well combined. Form into a ball and wrap with plastic wrap. Refrigerate overnight.

2   Divide the dough into 3 parts. Roll out one part of the dough as thin as possible, using flour to prevent sticking (don't add too much flour or the dough will become too hard).

3   Using the rim of a drinking glass or round cookie cutter, cut 2½-inch circles from the dough. Stretch each circle and place a teaspoonful of desired filling (see below) in the center. Fold dough over to form a half circle. With wet fingertips, pinch edges together very well.

4   For cheese filling, combine all ingredients. The filling will yield more than necessary for one batch of kreplach.

5   For chicken filling, sauté liver in oil with paprika, salt, and black pepper. Chop the liver and chicken into small pieces. Add egg and combine.   ▶

6 Fill an 8-quart pot with 6 quarts water and a drop of oil. Bring water to a boil. Add up to 20 kreplach into the hot water. Stir and swirl kreplach around with a spoon. When the water boils again, lower the heat. Cover and cook for 20 minutes. Pour out most of the hot water and add cold water to the pot to cover kreplach to chill. Drain the kreplach in a colander. Toss the drained kreplach in oil to prevent sticking.

7 For chicken kreplach, add to soup and serve.

8 For cheese kreplach, dip each filled krepel into breadcrumbs and fry on both sides. Kreplach will fry in very little oil or butter. Sprinkle with confectioner's sugar.

SQUARE DOUGHNUTS

YIELD APPROXIMATELY
24 DOUGHNUTS

4 CUPS	FLOUR
1/4 CUP	SUGAR
2 1/4 TSP	DRY YEAST
2	EGGS
1 1/4 CUP	WARM WATER
PINCH	SALT
1/4 CUP (1/2 STICK)	MARGARINE, AT ROOM TEMPERATURE
•	OIL, FOR FRYING

Why do we eat doughnuts on Chanukah? The Mishnah (*Keilim* 5:1) mentions *sufganah* (Hebrew for donut), whose root word is *sfog*, which means to absorb, like a sponge. What should it absorb? Oil, to commemorate the miracle of the oil that burned for eight days.

Forget about baked doughnuts this year, because these are heaven. When I went in search of a great doughnut recipe, I had two requirements. It had to still taste good more than an hour after frying, and it had to be so easy I wouldn't need to pull out my mixer. This recipe satisfies both. I make them square so that I don't waste any dough! Who decided doughnuts have to be round, anyway?

Make sure you use enough oil so that your doughnuts will be fully deep fried and won't overcrowd the pot. Too many donuts at once will lower the temperature of the oil and prevent them from cooking properly.

1   In a large bowl, combine the flour, sugar, yeast, eggs and warm water. Mix with a wooden spoon. Add the salt and incorporate it into the dough. Cut the margarine into small pieces and add to the bowl. Knead the dough by hand. (You may need to add a bit of flour, but use as little as possible. A sticky dough yields a fluffier doughnut.) Knead for a minimum of 5 minutes.

2   Cover the dough and let rise for 2 hours in a warm, draft-free spot. ▶

3 Sprinkle flour over the rolling surface. Place the dough onto the flour, and then sprinkle additional flour over the dough. Roll the dough out in the shape of a half-inch-thick rectangle. (At this point you may add as much flour as you need to ensure that the dough won't stick to the rolling surface.)

4 Using a knife or a pizza cutter, cut squares about 2½ x 2½ inches. Separate the squares; sprinkle with additional flour if necessary. Cover and let rise for 45 minutes.

5 Heat oil over medium-high heat for 10 minutes before frying. (Optional: Using your thumb, punch a hole right through the center of the doughnut.) Slip into hot oil. Fry in batches of 3 or 4 at a time. Sprinkle with confectioner's sugar.

NOTE

Heating a large amount of oil can take a long time. Deep-frying should be done with the oil at 325°F (185°C). Use a candy thermometer that you can hook onto the side of the pot.

If you don't have a thermometer, try these tricks:

- Place a kernel of popcorn in the oil. When it pops, the oil is ready.

- The most common way to test the oil is to drop in one piece of dough. If it doesn't bubble the oil is not yet hot enough. If it browns too quickly, the oil is too hot.

- Don't feel that you must use a huge pot of oil when frying. A small pot conserves oil, allows it to heat faster, and produces the same results.

No matter what the temperature, overcrowding the pot will result in dramatic temperature changes and will result in oily food. Be sure oil remains at the proper temperature.

SAVORY HAMENTASHEN & APRICOT DIPPING SAUCE

YIELD 12-15 HAMENTASHEN

4 (10-INCH CIRCLES)	**FROZEN MALAWAH DOUGH**
2 TBSP	**HONEY**
3 CLOVES	**GARLIC**
1 FULL TBSP	**SALT**
2 TBSP	**SOY SAUCE**
2 TBSP	**APPLE JUICE**
3	**CHICKEN CUTLETS,** CUBED
¼ CUP	**RED BELL PEPPER,** FINELY DICED
•	**OIL, FOR FRYING**

APRICOT DIPPING SAUCE

1 CUP	**APRICOT JAM**
2 TBSP	**MUSTARD**
2 TBSP	**SOY SAUCE**
1 TBSP	**HONEY**

On Purim day, who wouldn't love something they can serve at the festive meal instead of more candy?

1 In a medium bowl, combine honey, garlic, salt, soy sauce, and apple juice. Marinate chicken in mixture for a minimum of 30 minutes. Add the diced red pepper.

2 Remove malawah dough from freezer to begin defrosting.

3 When dough has slightly defrosted (approximately 10 minute after removing from freezer), use a cookie cutter to cut out 2¼-inch circles. Defrost circles for an additional 5 minutes. Using a rolling pin or pressing down with your hands, roll the dough circles slightly until they are 3½ inches wide.

4 Place a heaping teaspoonful of chicken mixture into the center of each circle. Pinch the edges together to form a hamentash.

5 Heat a thin layer of oil in a skillet or frying pan. Add hamentashen to pan, filled side down. Fry over medium-low heat for 10-12 minutes, flipping halfway through or until golden (the heat needs to be low enough so the chicken is cooked before the dough browns).

6 To prepare dipping sauce, add all ingredients to a bowl and stir to combine thoroughly.

7 Serve hamentashen warm with dipping sauce.

STUFFED CABBAGE

1 CUP	**RICE**
1 LARGE HEAD	**GREEN CABBAGE**
•	**WATER,** AS NEEDED
3 TBSP	**OIL,** DIVIDED
1	**ONION**
1 LB	**CHOPPED MEAT**
•	**SALT AND PEPPER,** TO TASTE

SAUCE

3 TBSP	**OIL**
2	**ONIONS,** DICED
½ TSP	**SALT**
1 QUART	**TOMATO JUICE**
1 CUP	**WATER**
3 TBSP	**SUGAR**
•	**PEPPER,** TO TASTE

This is my grandmother's method for making stuffed cabbage.

1 Soak rice overnight in cold water.

2 Bring a 6-quart pot of water to a boil. Insert cabbage, root side down, and turn off the heat. Leave cabbage in the hot water for 10-15 minutes. Remove; allow to cool.

3 Meanwhile, heat 2 Tablespoon oil in a skillet over medium heat. Add the onion and sauté until soft.

4 When cabbage has softened, remove from pot. Using a knife, cut out the root, carving around it in a circle. Be careful not to tear the leaves.

5 Drain the rice and add to chopped meat. Add sautéed onion, salt, and pepper and mix well.

6 To stuff the cabbage, position a leaf with the cut side toward you. Place a large spoonful of meat in the bottom center of the leaf. Fold the bottom of the leaf over the meat. Fold in the sides over the center and roll up tightly. If the cabbage tears, use another leaf to cover and patch. Repeat with remaining leaves.

7 In a large sauté pan, prepare the sauce. Heat the oil over medium heat. Add onions and salt; cook till onions are translucent. Add tomato juice, water, sugar, and seasoning and bring to a boil. Lower heat and add cabbage, packing tightly, up to 2 layers high. Return to a boil. Reduce heat to medium and cook, covered, for 1½ hours. Taste and adjust seasoning.

FREEZER TIPS

WRAPPING AND STORING

The first rule is, "First in, first out." Rotate foods so that you use the older items first and enjoy your food at its prime.

HERE ARE SOME ADDITIONAL IMPORTANT TIPS:

- Most importantly, wrap your food properly.

- Use high-quality containers, such as Tupperware or Rubbermaid, for food that will be kept frozen for an extended period.

- Use square containers — they are easy to stack and take up less room than round or oval containers.

- Ice cube trays are the perfect molds for freezing small portions of pesto, tomato paste, etc. Once they are frozen solid, the cubes can be transferred to a resealable freezer bag for safekeeping.

- Freeze foods with parchment paper between layers so that you can easily remove only as much as you want.

- Freeze marinated and raw meat or chicken in ziptop bags. Then defrost in the refrigerator overnight. The meat will tenderize as it thaws.

- Running out of containers? Line a baking pan with foil and fill with contents. Use enough foil to wrap over the contents. Remove frozen foil-wrapped contents from pan and slide them into a ziplock bag. You can also place a bag into a container. Fill with desired food (soups work well). Freeze. Remove bag and reuse the container.

- Save space by placing soups into a freezer bag. Seal and place flat on freezer shelf. You can stack bags of frozen soup.

- Stack similar food items together. Designate separate areas or shelves for meat, cakes, doughs, breads, etc.

- Freeze food when it is fresh. The fresher it is when you freeze it, the better it will taste when defrosted.

DESSERTS

COLORFUL POPCORN

14 CUPS	**POPPED POPCORN**
2 CUPS	**SUGAR**
¼ CUP	**GEL DESSERT POWDER** (ABOUT ½ BOX)
½ CUP	**WATER**
1 TBSP	**OIL**
¼ TSP	**BAKING SODA**

Colorful popcorn is fun to prepare and fun to eat. If you plan on buying popcorn to prepare this recipe, be sure to purchase only white popcorn. Yellow popcorn is already artificially flavored and the pink or blue colors will be off (the orange popcorn, though, will work fine).

To package the popcorn, I used wide plastic 9 oz. tumblers and inserted them into cellophane bags, tied with a bow.

1 Preheat oven to 250°F.

2 Place the popped popcorn in a large bowl and set aside.

3 In a medium saucepan over high heat, combine the sugar, gel dessert powder, water, and oil. Bring to a boil. When liquid boils, cook it for 4 minutes without stirring (swirl the pot occasionally). Remove from heat and add baking soda. Pour over the popcorn and toss well to coat. Work quickly as the liquid will dry up.

4 Line two baking sheets with foil. Spread popcorn out on both pans. Bake for 1 hour. Stir occasionally.

5 Remove from oven and cool slightly before serving.

NOTE

PINK POPCORN
Use strawberry or cherry gel dessert powder.

ORANGE POPCORN
Use orange gel dessert powder with yellow store-bought popcorn.

BLUE POPCORN
Use berry or unflavored gel dessert powder with 3 drops of blue food coloring.

GREEN POPCORN
Use lime gel dessert powder. If the color is very light, you can add one drop of green food coloring.

JUMBO PINK-&-WHITE COOKIE

YIELD 1 LARGE CAKE-SIZED COOKIE

½ CUP (1 STICK)	MARGARINE
1 SCANT CUP	SUGAR
2	EGGS
¾ CUP	ORANGE JUICE
1 TSP	VANILLA SUGAR
2½ CUPS	FLOUR
1 TSP	BAKING POWDER
PINCH	SALT

ICING

⅓–½ CUP	BOILING WATER
1 LB	CONFECTIONER'S SUGAR
•	RED FOOD COLORING

Homemade birthday cakes are almost always better than bakery cakes, but most people I know aren't inclined to spend an entire afternoon piping flowers onto a sheet cake. I'm not either, and that's why I love this. It's colorful and my children appreciate it just as much.

1 Preheat oven to 325°F.

2 In the bowl of a mixer, cream the margarine and sugar. Add the eggs, orange juice and vanilla sugar. Mix well.

3 In a separate bowl, combine the flour, baking powder, and salt. Gradually add the dry ingredients to the mixer. Beat on low to combine.

4 Line a 12-inch pizza pan with parchment paper. Transfer the batter to the prepared pan, shaping it into a dome. Bake for 40 minutes or until cookie is firm. Cool completely in pan before icing. ▶

5 Prepare the icing by gradually stirring the boiling water into the confectioner's sugar to form a thick, spreadable mixture. Use as little water as possible (you can always add more later if the mixture is too thick).

6 Flip the cookie so that the flat side faces up. Cover half of the cookie with half of the frosting. Color the remaining icing with a few drops of red food coloring, stirring until it turns pink. Spread the pink frosting on the remaining half of the cookie.

7 Let the frosting set. When preparing in advance, cover well with foil, tenting foil over the cookie to prevent sticking. Keep frozen until an hour before serving.

NOTE

BLACK-&-WHITE VARIATION

To make a classic black-&-white cookie, in Step 6, coat half the cookie with half of the white frosting. Melt together 1 oz bittersweet baking chocolate with 1 teaspoon light corn syrup and remaining frosting. Stir in 1-2 teaspoons cocoa to achieve desired color. Spread the chocolate frosting on the remaining half of the cookie.

RAINBOW CUPCAKES

Rainbow cupcakes are perfect for a birthday girl or boy. They're so yum, you'll join in celebrating the milestone. If you're looking for a good basic cupcake recipe, try these without the food coloring.

YIELD 12 CUPCAKES

2½ CUPS	**FLOUR**
1½ CUPS	**SUGAR**
2 TBSP	**VANILLA SUGAR**
1 TBSP (+ 1 TSP)	**BAKING POWDER**
¾ CUP	**OIL**
1 CUP	**ORANGE JUICE**
2	**EGGS**
•	**RED, GREEN, AND BLUE FOOD COLORING**

1   Preheat oven to 350°F.

2   Sift together the flour, sugars, and baking powder. Add oil, orange juice, and eggs and mix until thoroughly combined.

3   Divide the batter into 4 bowls, one cup per bowl. Use food coloring to color 1 part red, 1 part green, 1 part blue, leaving 1 part plain.

4   Line a 12-cup cupcake pan with paper cupcake liners. Using a small scooper, place 1 scoop of each color into each cupcake liner. Bake for 25 minutes.

5   Remove from pan. Cool on rack. Decorate with frosting or whipped cream and sprinkles.

CHOCOLATE FUDGE SAUCE

Chocolate makes everything taste better! If you like coffee flavor, you can add an additional teaspoon of coffee. This chocolate sauce freezes well; simply rewarm over low heat.

YIELD 2½ CUPS

½ CUP (1 STICK)	**MARGARINE**
½ CUP	**BROWN SUGAR**
1¼ CUPS	**SUGAR**
1 8OZ CONTAINER	**NON-DAIRY WHIPPED TOPPING**
1 CUP	**COCOA**
2 TSP	**INSTANT COFFEE GRANULES**

1 In a medium saucepan, melt the margarine.

2 Remove from heat, add the remaining ingredients, and stir until well combined.

3 Serve warm over ice cream.

CHOCOLATE CHIP BISCOTTI

YIELD 30-34 BISCOTTI

3	EGGS
1¼ CUPS	SUGAR
1 CUP	OIL
1 TBSP	VANILLA SUGAR
4 CUPS	FLOUR
2 TSP	BAKING POWDER
8oz	CHOCOLATE CHIPS

TOPPING

2 TBSP	SUGAR
½ TSP	CINNAMON

Biscotti (roughly meaning "twice baked") are crisp Italian cookies often containing nuts or flavored with anise. Biscotti are made by shaping the dough into 2 long slabs, cutting the baked slabs into slices, then baking again to a crisp with the slices lying down.

Truthfully, there is one main difference between biscotti and mandelbrodt, whose literal translation is "almond bread," although, like biscotti, any nuts or ingredients can be incorporated. While traditional biscotti have very little butter (or oil) or none at all, mandelbrodt, its Jewish cousin, always contains plenty.

1 Preheat oven to 350°F.

2 In the bowl of a mixer on high speed, beat the eggs with sugar for 3-4 minutes. Add oil and vanilla sugar until well combined, approximately 2-3 minutes. Combine flour and baking powder. Add the flour mixture and chocolate chips, alternating between the two.

3 With wet hands, form dough into 2 loaves on a baking sheet lined with parchment paper. Combine topping ingredients; sprinkle evenly onto each loaf.

4 Bake for 30 minutes. Cool for approximately 10 minutes. Slice the loaves (see note on facing page) into ¾-inch-thick slices and place the biscotti on the baking sheet, one cut side down. Bake for an additional 5-8 minutes.

CHOCOLATE ALMOND BISCOTTI

PARVE

1 Preheat oven to 350°F.

2 In the bowl of a mixer, beat the oil and sugar at medium speed. Add eggs, vanilla sugar, and cocoa. Combine flour and baking powder. Gradually add the flour mixture and chocolate chips, alternating between the two. Do not over-mix. Fold in the almonds.

3 With wet hands, form the dough into 2 loaves on a baking sheet lined with parchment paper.

4 Bake for 30 minutes. Let cool. Slice the loaves (see note below) and place the biscotti on the baking sheet, one cut side down. Bake for an additional 10 minutes (or 4-5 minutes on each side).

YIELD 20 BISCOTTI

⅓ CUP	OIL
⅔ CUP	SUGAR
2	EGGS
1 TSP	VANILLA SUGAR
⅓ CUP	COCOA
1¾ CUP	FLOUR
2 TSP	BAKING POWDER
½ CUP	SEMISWEET CHOCOLATE CHIPS
¼ CUP	TOASTED ALMONDS, SLIVERED OR SLICED

NOTE

SLICING THE BISCOTTI

When shaping loaves, always use wet hands. The length is a personal choice. Some people love short biscotti while others prefer longer ones. Loaves can be anywhere between 5-7 inches long. After cooling loaves, cut with a serrated knife into ⅓–1½-inch-thick slices. Again, it's a personal choice. Slicing biscotti evenly and thinly takes some practice, but no matter how you slice it, the biscotti will look and taste great.

EVERYTHING BUT THE KITCHEN SINK COOKIES

PARVE

YIELD 16 JUMBO COOKIES

1 CUP (2 STICKS)	**MARGARINE**
1 CUP	**SUGAR**
1 CUP	**BROWN SUGAR**
1 TBSP	**VANILLA SUGAR**
2	**EGGS**
1½ CUPS	**FLOUR**
1 TSP	**BAKING POWDER**
PINCH	**SALT**
1 CUP	**PECANS,** COARSELY CHOPPED
2 CUPS	**QUICK COOKING** OR **OLD-FASHIONED OATS**
3½ OZ	**GOOD QUALITY CHOCOLATE,** COARSELY CHOPPED
1 CUP	**CHOCOLATE CHIPS**

In 1937, Ruth Wakefield was baking chocolate butter cookies for her guests at the Tollhouse Inn in Massachusetts. She was out of baking chocolate and short on time, so she quickly chopped up a semi-sweet chocolate bar and mixed it with the dough, expecting the chocolate to melt during baking and turn the cookies chocolaty brown. They didn't — and the rest is history. Ruth's chocolate chunk cookies became so popular, she shared the recipe with Nestlé in exchange for a lifetime supply of chocolate. Two years later, Nestlé created the first chocolate morsels, and it was no longer necessary to chop up a bar. In this recipe, we go back to the original method and use a bar of good quality chocolate. I like to keep these cookies in the freezer and warm one up in the microwave when I want to treat myself. There's so much stuff in these — who needs a meal?

1 Preheat oven to 350°F.

2 In the bowl of a mixer, cream the margarine and sugars. Gradually add the eggs.

3 In a separate bowl, sift together the flour, baking powder, and salt. Turn the mixer to low and add the flour mixture to the batter. Gradually add the pecans, oats, chopped chocolate, and chocolate chips.

4 Using an ice cream scoop, form balls. Place up to 6 balls on a parchment-lined baking sheet, allowing space for them to spread. Bake for 19-21 minutes.

NOTE

WHAT'S THE DIFFERENCE BETWEEN A SOFT COOKIE AND A CRISPY ONE?

Soft cookies are baked at a higher temperature for a shorter baking time. They have a lower fat-to-flour ratio. Margarine is often melted before mixing, there are more eggs, and a higher ratio of brown sugar vs. white. In addition, if you refrigerate the dough it takes longer for the butter or margarine to melt, resulting in softer cookies.

Crispier cookies bake at a lower temperature for a longer baking time. They have a higher fat-to-flour ratio and usually include margarine that is not melted first. The simplest way to crisp up your chocolate chip cookie is to up the white sugar and reduce the brown.

QUICK & EASY PECAN BARS

This is a quick version of a pecan pie, which can be cut into triangles or rectangles. Serve two pieces on a dessert plate with a scoop of vanilla ice cream between them. Add a warm pecan sauce, and your family or company will feel really indulged.

YIELD 20-24 BARS

CRUST

½ CUP (1 STICK)	**MARGARINE**
½ CUP	**BROWN SUGAR**
1	**EGG YOLK**
1½ CUPS	**FLOUR**

PECAN FILLING

1 CUP	**BROWN SUGAR**
½ CUP (1 STICK)	**MARGARINE**
4 TBSP	**HONEY**
½ CUP	**NON-DAIRY WHIPPED TOPPING**
3 CUPS	**CHOPPED PECANS**
DASH	**SALT**

WARM PECAN SAUCE

1 CUP	**BROWN SUGAR**
1 8OZ CONTAINER	**NON-DAIRY WHIPPED TOPPING**
½ CUP	**WHOLE PECANS**

1 Preheat oven to 350°F.

2 Line a 9x13-inch pan with parchment paper. Combine the crust ingredients and press evenly into the pan. Bake for 15 minutes or until golden brown.

3 To prepare the filling, in a small saucepan, combine the brown sugar, margarine, and honey. Bring to a boil. Add the whipped topping, pecans, and salt. Pour this mixture over the baked crust. Bake for 30-35 minutes. Remove the pan from the oven and let cool. Cut into 1x3-inch bars or desired shape.

4 In a small saucepan over medium heat, prepare the warm pecan sauce. Combine the brown sugar, whipped topping, and whole pecans. Cook until the sugar dissolves. Serve warm over ice cream.

HEALTHY PEANUT BUTTER BARS

PARVE

YIELD 12 SQUARES

½ CUP	OIL
½ CUP	CHUNKY PEANUT BUTTER
½ CUP	SUGAR
½ CUP	BROWN SUGAR
1 TBSP	VANILLA SUGAR
1	EGG
½ CUP	WHITE WHOLE WHEAT FLOUR
½ CUPS	OLD FASHIONED OATS
½ TSP	BAKING SODA
DASH	SALT
⅓ CUP	CHOCOLATE CHIPS

This is for Rivky who wanted peanut butter cookies. Bars are easier and quicker and these have a great crispy crunch (especially the end pieces).

1 Preheat oven to 350°F.

2 In the bowl of a stand mixer, combine oil, peanut butter, and sugars. Mix on high speed until thoroughly combined. Gradually add egg, flour, oats, baking soda, salt, and chocolate chips.

3 Line a 9x13-inch pan with parchment paper. Press batter very well into pan. Bake for 40 minutes.

4 Let cool and cut into squares.

WHAT'S WHITE WHOLE WHEAT FLOUR?

White whole wheat flour is milled using "white" or albino wheat rather than the traditional red wheat. Like the whole wheat flour we're accustomed to, it retains many more nutrients than the traditionally bleached white flour. This type of flour produces baked goods that taste as if they were made with regular all-purpose flour, so it is often considered the ideal compromise between taste and proper nutrition. It is best used for cookies and cakes.

OATMEAL CHOCOLATE-CHIP COOKIES

YIELD 8 COOKIES

½ CUP	OIL
⅓ CUP	SUGAR
⅓ CUP	BROWN SUGAR
1	EGG
¾ CUP	FLOUR
PINCH	SALT
½ TSP	BAKING POWDER
1 TBSP	VANILLA SUGAR
1¼ CUPS	OLD-FASHIONED OATS
¾ CUP	CHOCOLATE CHIPS

I receive complaints from people all the time when the recipes I publish aren't healthy enough. Many people have a specific vendetta against margarine. To me, margarine is a necessary ingredient in cookies, but for those who prefer to bake without it, I created this recipe.

1 Preheat oven to 350°F.

2 In the bowl of a mixer, beat the oil, sugar, and brown sugar on low speed. Add the egg. Whisk together the flour, salt, baking powder, and vanilla sugar. Add mixture to the batter. Gradually add the oats and chocolate chips.

3 Press the batter into a round 10-inch pan. Bake for 30-35 minutes.

4 Let cool. Cut into 8 triangles, like a pizza.

JAM PIE

I recently received a beautiful pecan brownie cake presented on a charger. The cake was made in a low tart pan and it fit onto the charger perfectly. (Most chargers are about 13 inches total in diameter, with a 9-inch diameter interior.) I thought this was a very nice idea, so I phoned my friend and asked if I could steal it. Then, I simplified even more by making an easy jam pie.

Acrylic chargers look great and can be purchased at closeout stores for a dollar or two. They're also available in bulk online from restaurant supply stores in almost every color. All you need is a bow to tie it up.

YIELD 2 9-INCH AND 1 8-INCH PIE (OR 3 9-INCH PIES WITH A THINNER CRUST)

DOUGH

1¾–2 CUPS	**FLOUR**
½ CUP	**SUGAR**
½ CUP (1 STICK)	**MARGARINE**
1	**EGG**
APPROX. ¾ CUP	**STRAWBERRY JAM** OR YOUR FAVORITE FLAVOR

CRUMBLE

1 CUP	**FLOUR**
½ CUP	**SUGAR**
½ CUP (1 STICK)	**MARGARINE**

1   Preheat oven to 350°F.

2   To prepare dough, combine 1¾ cup flour, sugar, margarine, and egg. Knead until dough forms. Reserve the extra ¼ cup flour to use sparingly if dough is too moist. The dough consistency should be slightly crumbly. Line 3 9-inch round pans with parchment paper. Press dough into the pans to form the crust. (The dough usually yields 2 9-inch and 1 8-inch, but it depends on how thin you press it in.)

3   Spread strawberry jam on the dough.

4   Combine crumble ingredients. Sprinkle over the jam.

5   Bake for 25-30 minutes. Cool completely before serving. (Freezes well.)

6   Alternatively, you can present by cutting into squares or triangles.

CHERRY POCKETS

YIELD 12 POCKETS

DOUGH

2 CUPS	**FLOUR**
½ CUP (1 STICK)	**MARGARINE**
¾ CUP	**SUGAR**
1	**EGG**
DASH	**SALT**

CHERRY FILLING

2 CUPS (12oz PACKAGE)	**FROZEN DARK SWEET CHERRIES**
⅓ CUP	**SUGAR**
2 TBSP	**FLOUR**
¼ TSP	**CINNAMON**
•	**CONFECTIONER'S SUGAR, FOR DUSTING**

For less fuss, you can make this as one big cherry pie. You will need to double the filling.

1 Preheat oven to 350°F.

2 Wetting hands slightly, combine flour, margarine, sugar, egg, and salt to form a dough.

3 Slightly defrost cherries. Mix with sugar, flour, and cinnamon.

4 Divide the dough in four and roll out one piece at a time. Using drinking glasses with different-sized rims or 2 cookie cutters, cut out twelve 3⅓-inch circles and twelve 2¾-inch circles.

5 Place 1 Tablespoon of cherry filling on one of the smaller dough circles. Cover with a larger circle and press edges down well. Repeat with remaining circles.

6 Bake pockets for 20-25 minutes, or large pies for 50-60 minutes.

7 The dough may crack slightly, giving it a nice color and rustic look.

8 Dust cooled pockets with confectioner's sugar.

NO-MIXER BROWNIE

YIELD 3 1-LB LOAF PANS OR 2 6X8-INCH PANS

2 CUPS	SUGAR
1¾ CUP	FLOUR
¾ CUP	COCOA
1½ TSP	BAKING POWDER
1½ TSP	BAKING SODA
1 TBSP	VANILLA SUGAR
3	EGGS
1 CUP	HOT WATER
½ CUP	OIL
1 8oz CONTAINER	NON-DAIRY WHIPPED TOPPING

My friend Chaya admitted that she has an aversion to her mixer. I hadn't developed any feelings toward mine, but as I pulled it out to bake a cake for Shabbos, I started to feel annoyed too. What a pain it is to pull a mixer out of its hiding place and wash all those parts when I'm done. The thought of using my mixer began to haunt me, so I decided to give it a hiatus. Chaya, please think carefully before you share your feelings on any other kitchen gadgets. I need them!

1 Preheat oven to 350°F.

2 In a bowl, combine the sugar, flour, cocoa, baking powder, baking soda, and vanilla sugar. Add the eggs, hot water, oil, and whipped topping and stir until batter is smooth.

3 Pour batter into 3 1-lb loaf pans or 2 6x8-inch pans.

4 Bake for 45-50 minutes.

ORANGE CAKE WITH CHOCOLATE GLAZE

This is an easy and quick bundt cake that is perfect for Shabbos morning.

BATTER

8	**EGGS,** SEPARATED
2 CUPS	**SUGAR**
2 CUPS	**FLOUR**
1 TBSP	**VANILLA SUGAR**
1 TSP	**BAKING POWDER**
½ CUP	**OIL**
¾ CUP	**ORANGE JUICE**
1 TSP	**ORANGE ZEST,** OPTIONAL

GLAZE

8oz	**BITTERSWEET CHOCOLATE**
6 TBSP	**NON-DAIRY WHIPPED TOPPING**
6 TBSP	**CORN SYRUP**

1 Preheat oven to 350°F. Thoroughly grease and flour a 12-cup bundt pan.

2 Beat the egg whites until stiff peaks form. Gradually add the sugar, yolks, and remaining batter ingredients.

3 Pour batter into bundt pan and bake for 60-70 minutes. Allow to cool slightly (about 5 minutes) and quickly invert onto rack until cold. The cake will be more difficult to remove if left in the pan until cold.

4 To prepare glaze, place all the glaze ingredients into a pot. Cook over low heat, stirring until combined.

5 Transfer cooled cake to serving platter. Pour warm glaze over the cake, allowing it to drizzle down the sides.

CHOCOLATE BABKA

DOUGH

6¾ TSP	DRY OR 2oz FRESH YEAST
½ CUP	WARM WATER
6½ CUPS	FLOUR
½ CUP	SUGAR
1½ CUPS (3 STICKS)	MARGARINE
½ CUP	ORANGE JUICE, AT ROOM TEMPERATURE
4	EGGS
PINCH	SALT

FILLING

2 CUPS	SUGAR
½ CUP	CONFECTIONER'S SUGAR
1 CUP	COCOA, SIFTED
2 TBSP	COFFEE
1 TBSP	VANILLA SUGAR

One of my favorite memories growing up was smelling my mother's babka or rugelach baking. The aromas would meet me the moment I walked through the door. Now, I make the same recipe and it smells and tastes just as I remember.

1 In the bowl of a mixer fitted with a dough hook, dissolve the yeast in water with a bit of sugar. After yeast has bubbled, add the remaining dough ingredients. Mix well until the dough is smooth. Cover and allow to rise for 1 hour.

2 To prepare the filling, combine all ingredients in a small bowl. Set aside.

3 To prepare topping (see facing page), mix ingredients by hand to form coarse crumbs.

4 Preheat oven to 350°F. Grease the pans.

5 To assemble babka, divide dough into 3 pieces. Work with 1 piece at a time. Roll out the dough to double the length of the pan (about the size of a baking sheet) and smear with oil. Spread ⅓ of the chocolate filling over the dough. Roll up jellyroll style and pinch the ends closed. Fold the roll in half and twist 3 times. Transfer to the loaf pan. Brush with the beaten egg. Sprinkle the streusel topping over the entire roll. Repeat with the remaining 2 pieces of dough.

6 Bake for 1 hour.

STREUSEL TOPPING

½ CUP (1 STICK)	**MARGARINE**
½ CUP	**SUGAR**
1½ CUPS	**FLOUR**
1 TBSP	**VANILLA SUGAR**

TO ASSEMBLE

•	**OIL FOR SMEARING**
1	**EGG,** BEATEN, FOR EGG WASH

NOTE

DEEP CHOCOLATE FILLING VARIATION

3	**EGG WHITES**
2½ CUPS	**SUGAR**
½ CUP (1 STICK)	**MARGARINE**
1 TSP	**VANILLA SUGAR**
1 CUP	**COCOA**

1 Beat all ingredients together in a mixer bowl for 1-2 minutes on medium speed.

2 Spread over one piece of dough at a time. Proceed as above.

CHOCOLATE CRISPY TART

YIELD 8-10 SERVINGS

TART SHELL:

¾ CUP	MARGARINE, AT ROOM TEMPERATURE
½ CUP	SUGAR
2 HEAPING TBSP	COCOA
½ TSP	VANILLA EXTRACT
1¾ CUPS	FLOUR
PINCH	SALT

CHOCOLATE FILLING AND GANACHE:

3 3oz (100 GRAM)	BARS BITTERSWEET CHOCOLATE, DIVIDED
1 CUP	NON-DAIRY WHIPPED TOPPING, DIVIDED
2	EGGS, BEATEN
2 TBSP	FLOUR
DASH	SALT
1 TSP	MARGARINE

CRUNCH

1 TBSP	MARGARINE
2 TBSP	CORN SYRUP
2½ TBSP	SUGAR
1 CUP	COCOA CRISPIES CEREAL

Because of the crunch factor, I prefer nuts in all chocolate desserts, but some people don't like nuts and some are allergic to them, so I developed this recipe. You can make the crunch in advance and store in an air-tight container or in the freezer until ready to use. It tastes just great over ice cream, too.

1 To make the tart shell, beat the margarine and sugar in the bowl of a stand mixer. Add the cocoa and salt; beat well. Add the extract. Gradually add most of the flour. (I reserve ½ cup flour to incorporate by hand.)

2 Press the dough into a 9- or 10-inch tart pan with a removable bottom. You won't need the entire dough, about ¾ will be enough. Cover and refrigerate overnight.

3 Preheat oven to 350°F.

4 Set aside ⅓ cup whipped topping and ½-bar of chocolate for the ganache, below.

5 To make the chocolate filling, using a double boiler or microwaving in 20-second increments, melt 2½ bars of chocolate and remaining ⅔ cup whipped topping.

6 Beat egg yolks with a fork. Quickly whisk them into the double boiler, stirring well. Add the flour and salt. Pour into the tart shell.

7 Bake for 30 minutes. ▶

8   To make the chocolate ganache, using the remaining chocolate and whipped topping, melt the chocolate, whipped topping, and margarine in the microwave in 30-second increments. It won't look melted, but if you whisk it with a fork it will mix well. You can add a splash of chocolate liquor if you wish.

9   To make the crunch, preheat oven to 350°F.

10 In a small saucepan over medium heat, combine the margarine, corn syrup, and sugar. Cook until mixture turns golden brown, watching carefully.

11 Remove from heat and add the cereal. Spread mixture on a baking sheet lined with parchment paper and bake for 8-10 minutes. Let cool for 5 minutes.

12 Blend in a food processor for 2-3 seconds. Don't grind it too fine.

13 Spread the ganache over the tart and sprinkle with crunch. wrap well and freeze till firm. Defrost ½-1 hour before serving.

DEVORAH'S APRICOT TART

Devorah is the person I call when I'm in a pinch and need a quick recipe idea. Her recipes are always quick, easy, and delicious. Devorah makes this favorite all summer long using fresh apricots. You can use canned apricots the rest of the year for a little taste of summer.

YIELD 8 SERVINGS

DOUGH

4 TBSP (½ STICK)	**MARGARINE**
¾ CUP	**SUGAR**
3	**EGGS**
¼ CUP	**ORANGE JUICE**
¾ CUP	**OIL**
1½ CUPS	**FLOUR**
¼ TSP	**BAKING POWDER**
1 30oz CAN	**APRICOT HALVES IN SYRUP,** DRAINED WELL
•	**VANILLA SUGAR,** FOR SPRINKLING

1 Preheat the oven to 350°F.

2 In the bowl of a mixer, cream the margarine and sugar. Add the eggs, orange juice, oil, flour and baking powder. Pour the batter into a low 11-inch tart pan.

3 Pat dry the apricot halves, and position along the entire top of the batter. Sprinkle vanilla sugar over the top.

4 Bake for 45 minutes. Serve warm.

NOTE

If you are using a 9-inch tart pan, pour in ¾ of the batter and save the rest for an individual pie.

CINNAMON TWISTS

1 CUP	LUKEWARM WATER
¼ CUP	SUGAR
2oz	FRESH YEAST OR 6¾ TSP DRY YEAST
7½ CUPS	FLOUR
4	EGG YOLKS
1	EGG
1½ CUPS (3 STICKS)	MARGARINE
¼ TSP	SALT
1 CUP	ORANGE JUICE

FILLING

1 CUP	BROWN SUGAR
3 TSP	CINNAMON
½ CUP (1 STICK)	MARGARINE, MELTED

WARM PECAN SAUCE

1 CUP	BROWN SUGAR
1 8oz CONTAINER	NON-DAIRY WHIPPED TOPPING
½ CUP	WHOLE PECANS

Four years ago, Raizy Spitz, a phenomenal baker and cook, shared her recipe for Cinnamon Twists. It proved to be the ultimate winter dessert, and I have no idea why I never shared it with everyone until now.

1   In a mixer or large bowl, combine water, sugar, and yeast. Allow yeast to dissolve in the liquid. Add the remaining twist ingredients and mix until a smooth dough forms. (If the dough is too sticky, add one additional Tablespoon of flour at a time.) Transfer the dough to a bowl and cover. Let rise for 1 hour.

2   Preheat oven to 375°F.

3   To prepare filling, combine brown sugar and cinnamon. Set aside.

4   To assemble the twists, divide the dough into three parts. Roll one part to about the size of a baking sheet. Spread ⅓ of the margarine over the surface of the dough. Sprinkle ⅓ of the filling over the margarine. Fold the dough lengthwise in half. Cut into 10-12 strips along the length, and then cut each strip in half across the width.   ▶

5 Twist each strip to form a twist. Pinch the ends closed and place onto a baking sheet lined with parchment paper.

6 Bake for 15-18 minutes. Don't overbake, as the twists, served warm, will need to be heated again before serving. If serving at room temperature, bake for 2-3 additional minutes. Repeat with remaining dough and filling.

7 To prepare warm pecan sauce, combine all ingredients in a saucepan or in a micro-wave-safe container. Cook until melted and stir until thoroughly combined. Spoon over ice cream and warm twists.

DEEP-DISH CHOCOLATE CHIP PIES

PARVE

YIELD 6-8 SERVINGS

1 CUP (2 STICKS)	**MARGARINE**
¾ CUP	**LIGHT BROWN SUGAR**
¾ CUP	**SUGAR**
1 TBSP	**VANILLA SUGAR**
2	**EGGS**
DASH	**SALT**
3 CUPS	**FLOUR**
1 TSP	**BAKING POWDER**
1 CUP	**CHOCOLATE CHIPS**

Show me a recipe that includes chocolate chips, and I'll always find the time to try it. This one is just too good not to share. If you find chocolate chips dull, chop up a bar of Rosemary chocolate, add it to the batter, and call it a party. If you are going to serve this on Friday night, don't leave the pies sitting on the hot plate for very long, or they will dry out. Warm them up a few minutes before serving. Number of servings depends on the size of your ramekins.

1 Preheat oven to 375°F.

2 In the bowl of a mixer, cream the margarine and sugars until smooth. Add the eggs. In a second bowl, whisk together flour, salt, and baking powder. Add to the mixer and mix to incorporate. Add in the chocolate chips.

3 Transfer the batter to ramekins, filling halfway. Bake for 16-20 minutes, or until tops just start to turn golden brown; they should be slightly underbaked.

4 Serve warm.

NOTE

These little pies are even better topped with a scoop of vanilla ice cream.

HOT CHOCOLATE MOLTEN CAKE

PARVE

YIELD 4 SERVINGS

4oz	**GOOD QUALITY BITTERSWEET CHOCOLATE**
½ CUP	**OIL**
1 CUP	**SUGAR**
2	**EGGS**
2	**EGG YOLKS**
6 TBSP	**FLOUR**

Some desserts leave me speechless.

On Pesach, substitute potato starch for the flour for fabulous results. I also like to exchange the sugar for confectioner's sugar.

1 Preheat the oven to 425°F.

2 Thoroughly grease 4 individual glass ovensafe cups or a muffin pan.

3 In a double boiler, melt the chocolate with the oil. Remove from heat. Cool slightly

4 With a fork or a whisk, stir in the sugar until well blended. Beat the eggs and egg yolks with a fork; quickly add to the double boiler. Add the flour, stirring constantly. Pour into the prepared cups and bake for 13-15 minutes.

5 Remove from the oven. Let stand for 1 minute. Invert onto a plate.

NOTE

When are the molten cakes ready? The center of the top should still feel soft and jiggly, while the rim should be firm, like a cake. Serve this dessert right after baking. If it is reheated, the center will dry out.

CHOCOLATE CIGARS

BROWNIE CAKE

1⅓ CUPS	FLOUR
2 CUPS	SUGAR
¾ CUP	COCOA
½ TSP	SALT
1 TSP	BAKING POWDER
⅔ CUP	OIL
4	EGGS
2 TSP	VANILLA EXTRACT
¾ CUP	CHOPPED GLAZED PECANS, OPTIONAL
1 TSP	SALT
14-16	SPRING ROLL WRAPPERS

CORNSTARCH GLUE:

2 TBSP	CORNSTARCH
3 TBSP	WATER
	OIL FOR FRYING

Spring rolls are essentially very similar to egg rolls except they don't contain egg in the batter. Without the egg, they are thinner and crispier and really are much tastier than egg roll wrappers. If you can't find spring roll wrappers, you can use cigar wrappers.

1 Preheat oven to 350°F. Have 2 2-lb loaf pans ready.

2 Place the flour, sugar, cocoa, salt, and baking powder in a large bowl. Mix well with a fork. Add the wet ingredients and stir to combine. Do not overmix.

3 Divide the batter in half (about 1½ cups each). You can stir ¾ cup pecans into one half and the salt in the other half. Alternatively, you can leave it plain or double the nuts so that both have nuts. Pour one batter into each loaf pan. Bake for 35 to 40 minutes. Let cool.

4 Whisk the cornstarch and water together in a bowl.

5 Slice each cake into 8-10 slices. Place a spring roll wrapper on your work surface in a diamond shape. Place one strip of cake toward the lower edge. Since the cake is very moist, you can shape it a bit so that the cigar filling is evenly distributed. Roll the bottom corner over the cake tightly. Tuck both ends in and continue rolling the spring roll tightly. When you get to the end, brush the ends with the cornstarch glue so that it won't unroll during frying.

▶

6 In a small pot, heat the oil. Slip the spring roll into the oil. Fry on each side for about 1-2 minutes, until the spring roll crisps up and is golden brown. Remove and drain on paper towels.

7 Serve immediately with ice cream or whipped cream.

NOTE

Cigar wrappers are Middle Eastern wraps that are used to make Moroccan cigars. They are very similar to spring rolls and are imported, frozen, from Israel.

LAYERED PLUM CRISP

PARVE

YIELD 10-12 SERVINGS

CRUMBS

3 CUPS	FLOUR
1½ CUPS	SUGAR
1 TSP	VANILLA SUGAR
¾ CUP	OIL
1	EGG
1 TSP	BAKING POWDER

FILLING

4½ CUPS	PLUM SLICES
1½ TBSP	LEMON JUICE
3 TBSP	SUGAR

When purchasing plums, avoid those those are excessively hard. They are immature and will probably not develop a good taste and texture. Plums that yield to gentle pressure and are slightly soft at their tips are ripe and ready to be eaten. They should also be free of bruises or signs of decay.

1. Preheat oven to 350°F.

2. Place the crumb ingredients in a large bowl. Mix until crumbs form and set aside.

3. Mix plums with lemon juice and sugar.

4. Divide the crumbs into 3 equal parts (about 1¾ cup crumbs for each part). In a 9x13-inch pan, layer crumbs, half of the plums, crumbs, second half of the plums, and remaining crumbs.

5. Bake for 60-75 minutes.

NOTE

This is delicious when served hot, but yields messy portions. Let it sit a bit and serve warm, making it easier to slice.

TOWERING APPLE PIE

This apple pie needs no introduction. It's better than all the rest I have tried, and the leftovers are even better. Thanks, B. Friedman.

Do not use graham cracker pie crusts for this recipe.

YIELD 8 SERVINGS

1	**FRESH** OR **FROZEN 9-INCH PIE CRUST** OR **2 SMALLER PIE CRUSTS**

CRUMBS

½ CUP + 2 TBSP	**FLOUR**
½ CUP	**BROWN SUGAR**
⅓ CUP	**SUGAR**
½ TSP	**CINNAMON**
½ CUP (1 STICK)	**MARGARINE**

FILLING

5	**CORTLAND APPLES,** PEELED AND THINLY SLICED
1 TBSP	**LEMON JUICE**
½ CUP	**SUGAR**
3 TBSP	**FLOUR**
½ TSP	**CINNAMON**
⅛ TSP	**NUTMEG,** OPTIONAL

1 Preheat oven to 350°F. Prebake the pie crust(s) for 10-15 minutes.

2 Raise oven temperature to 450°F.

3 To prepare the crumb topping, combine all ingredients to form coarse crumbs. Set aside.

4 To prepare the apple filling, mix apple slices with remaining ingredients until they are well coated.

5 To assemble the pie, layer the apple slices into the prebaked pie crust, staggering the slices so they tower toward the center. Pat crumbs onto the apples to form top crust.

6 Place the pie in a large pan or on a baking sheet to catch the drips. Bake for 15 minutes at 450°F, then lower the temperature to 350°F and continue baking for 45 minutes.

CHEESE BUNS

These are a perfect personal size, so everyone can have one! They will freeze wonderfully in an airtight container or ziptop bag.

YIELD 40 BUNS

DOUGH

1½ oz	**FRESH YEAST**
¾ CUP	**VERY WARM WATER**
5 CUPS	**FLOUR**
½ CUP	**ORANGE JUICE**
1 CUP (2 STICKS)	**MARGARINE**
1	**EGG**
2	**EGGS,** SEPARATED
½ CUP	**SUGAR**
1 TBSP	**VANILLA SUGAR**

FILLING

1 LB	**WHIPPED CREAM CHEESE**
¾ CUP	**SUGAR**
1 TBSP	**VANILLA SUGAR**
1	**EGG,** SEPARATED
⅓ CUP	**CHOCOLATE CHIPS**

1 In the bowl of a mixer, combine the yeast with warm water. Sprinkle a bit of the sugar on this mixture and let stand until the yeast bubbles. Add the flour, juice, margarine, egg, egg yolks, sugar, and vanilla sugar. Mix well until a dough forms. Cover and let rise for 1 hour.

2 Preheat oven to 350°F.

3 To prepare filling, combine the cream cheese, sugar, vanilla sugar, and egg yolk.

4 Set aside egg whites for egg wash.

5 Divide the dough into 3-4 pieces. Working with one piece at a time, roll out each piece into a rectangle. Spread one-sixth of the filling over the dough and sprinkle it with chocolate chips. Roll up, jellyroll style, and slice into buns, about 2-3 fingers wide. Transfer the buns into the greased cups of a muffin pan (they need not entirely fill the indentation; the buns will grow as they bake). Brush with reserved egg whites.

6 Bake for 25-30 minutes, until golden. Remove from pan and cool on a rack.

NOTE

To make one large cheese babka, pile buns into a tube pan. Bake for 45 minutes.

CHEESE ROULADE

YIELD 12 SERVINGS

6	**EGGS,** SEPARATED
6 TBSP	**SUGAR**
5 TBSP	**FLOUR** + MORE FOR SPRINKLING
1 TBSP	**COCOA,** SIFTED
2 TSP	**OIL**

FILLING

6oz	**WHIPPED CREAM CHEESE,** ¾ CONTAINER
¾ CUP	**SUGAR**
1 3½ oz BAR	**MILK CHOCOLATE**

TOPPING

2 3½ oz BARS	**WHITE CHOCOLATE**
1 TSP	**INSTANT COFFEE GRANULES**
1–2 TBSP	**HOT WATER**

Using potato starch instead of flour, this is one of my favorite dairy Pesach desserts. When Chol Hamoed rolls around, and you've had enough of meat, serve this for breakfast or as a dessert after a dairy meal.

1   Preheat oven to 350°F.

2   In the bowl of a mixer, beat egg whites, gradually adding sugar, until peaks form. Fold in the yolks, flour, cocoa, and oil. Pour batter onto a baking sheet lined with parchment paper. Bake for 20 minutes.

3   While cake is baking, spread out a clean kitchen towel on the counter and sprinkle with flour. Invert hot cake onto the prepared towel and carefully peel off the parchment paper. Starting from one short edge, roll up the cake and the towel together, jellyroll style. Set aside and let cool.

4   To prepare filling, mix the whipped cream cheese and sugar until well combined. Set aside. Over a double boiler, melt the bar of milk chocolate. Unroll the cake and spread with a layer of melted chocolate. Smear cream-cheese mixture over melted chocolate. Roll up cake.

5   In a double boiler, melt white chocolate with coffee granules dissolved in water. Pour over cake. Freeze.

6   To serve, defrost cake slightly, garnish with drizzled melted chocolate or hazelnuts, and slice.

FUDGE BROWNIE CHEESECAKE

YIELD 12 SERVINGS

FUDGE BROWNIE

¾ CUP	OIL
¾ CUP	SUGAR
2	EGGS
1 TBSP	VANILLA SUGAR
¾ CUP	FLOUR
5oz	BITTERSWEET BAKING CHOCOLATE, MELTED
½ CUP	CHOCOLATE CHIPS

CHEESE FILLING

4 (8oz) CONTAINERS	WHIPPED CREAM CHEESE (FOR A PAREVE CAKE, USE TOFUTTI BRAND)
4	EGGS
1¾ CUP	SUGAR
1 TBSP	VANILLA SUGAR
•	FOR PARVE CAKE: 1 TBSP LEMON JUICE

TWO TONE (OPTIONAL)

2oz	DARK MILK CHOCOLATE
2oz	BAKING CHOCOLATE

Fact #1: All cheesecakes are good. Fact #2: All fudge brownies are good. Cheesecake + Brownie = Out of this world delicious. This cheesecake actually gives you lots of options — you can go traditional, pareve, or knock it out with the two-tone version.

1   To prepare brownie crust, beat the oil, sugar, and eggs together for 10 minutes. Gradually add the vanilla sugar, flour, melted chocolate, and chocolate chips. Mix well. Pour the batter into a greased 9-inch or 10-inch springform pan. (I used a square pan)

2   To prepare filling, combine the cream cheese, eggs, and sugars and mix well. (If you use Tofutti cream cheese, add the lemon juice at this point.)

3   For a regular cheesecake, pour the filling over the crust. To create the two-tone cheesecake, divide the filling in half. Melt the chocolates together. Combine the melted chocolates with one half of the filling and pour over crust. Optionally, freeze for one hour.

4   Once firm, pour the plain cheesecake layer on top.

5   Preheat the oven to 350°F and position a 9x13-inch pan of cold water on the bottom rack to allow the steam to create a great environment for baking the delicate cheesecake. Place the cheesecake on the middle rack. Bake for 1½ hours.

NOTE

GARNISHING YOUR CAKE

To achieve the look depicted in the photo, freeze the cake for 30 minutes before garnishing.

Prepare a white chocolate glaze by melting a 3½-oz bar of good quality white milk chocolate; stir in 5-6 Tablespoons of heavy cream until you achieve a smooth, pourable glaze. Pour this over the cake. Cover the top of the cake entirely with chocolate candies, such as Kliks, creating a neat design. You will need about six packs of chocolate balls to decorate the entire surface. Alternatively, create a border with two rows around the perimeter of the cake.

BREAKFAST CHEESECAKE

YIELD 3 9" PIES, 8 SERVINGS EACH

1 LB	**FARMER CHEESE**
1½ CUPS	**SOUR CREAM** (¾ CONTAINER)
1 8oz CONTAINER	**WHIPPED CREAM CHEESE**
6	**EGGS,** SEPARATED
¼ CUP	**ORANGE JUICE**
1 TBSP	**VANILLA SUGAR**
1½ CUPS	**SUGAR,** DIVIDED
3	**9" ROUND GRAHAM CRACKER PIE SHELLS**
3 TBSP	**FLOUR,** HEAPING

SOUR CREAM TOPPING

1½ CUPS	**SOUR CREAM** (¾ CONTAINER)
1 TBSP	**VANILLA SUGAR**
1 TBSP	**SUGAR**

My mother serves this for breakfast every Shabbos morning, and my family polishes two cakes off completely. You can use reduced fat cream cheese and reduced fat sour cream for a lighter version. You can also serve this in a Pyrex baking dish or bake in a springform pan for a more elegant presentation. This is my daughter's favorite, as she says, "I loooovvve Bubbe's cheesecake."

Although the recipe makes three pies, this cheesecake freezes well, so simply wrap the extras (if there are any) and freeze to enjoy later.

1 Preheat oven to 350°F.

2 In a large bowl, using a spoon, mix farmer cheese, sour cream, and cream cheese. Add egg yolks, orange juice, vanilla sugar, and ¾ cup sugar. Mix until incorporated. Add flour.

3 In a mixer, beat egg whites until stiff peaks form. Gradually add the remaining ¾ cup sugar.

4 Fold beaten whites into the cheese mixture. Divide filling between the 3 pie shells. ▶

5 Bake for 40 minutes. The cheesecakes should be slightly golden on the edges.

6 To prepare topping, combine sour cream and sugars.

7 Remove cheesecakes from oven and let cool 5 minutes. When still warm, divide the sour cream topping between the three cheesecakes. With the back of a spoon, starting from the center, swirl the topping across the top until it covers the entire cake.

8 If serving for dessert, you can alternatively drizzle with dulce de leche, caramel, or desired topping.

FROZEN BLUEBERRY CRISP

YIELD 8-10 SERVINGS

56oz **VANILLA ICE CREAM,** SLIGHTLY SOFTENED

CRUMBLE

½ CUP **SUGAR**

½ CUP **FLOUR**

¼ CUP (½ STICK) **MARGARINE**

¼ CUP **SLICED ALMONDS**

BLUEBERRY SAUCE

1 (12oz) PACKAGE **FROZEN BLUEBERRIES**

1 TBSP **VANILLA SUGAR**

2 TBSP **WATER**

GARNISH

- **CONFECTIONER'S SUGAR**
- **FRESH BLUEBERRIES**

A while back I ate at an upscale restaurant and ordered a very similar dessert. I loved the surprise factor of it and decided to replicate it at home. It looks like a crisp, but as you dig your spoon in, you're rewarded with cold ice cream. It's best if you leave it out at room temperature for 10 minutes so that the ice cream has softened by the time you eat it.

1 Preheat oven to 350°F. To prepare the crumble, combine the sugar, flour, and margarine to form crumbs. Spread on a baking sheet lined with parchment paper. Bake for 15-25 minutes, stirring with a fork halfway through. Let cool and break into crumbles.

2 Preheat oven to 400°F. Toast the sliced almonds on a baking sheet for 8-10 minutes. Combine the prepared crumble with the toasted almonds.

3 To prepare the blueberry sauce, combine the blueberries, vanilla sugar, and water in a small saucepan. Cook over medium heat for 15-20 minutes. Using an immersion blender, thoroughly blend all ingredients.

4 To assemble blueberry crisps, place 1 scoop of vanilla ice cream into a ramekin. Top with 1 Tablespoon of blueberry sauce. Add a second scoop of ice cream and ½ Tablespoon of sauce. With the back of a spoon, smooth down the ice cream and sauce to create an even layer. Sprinkle with loads of crumble. Freeze.

5 To serve, garnish with confectioner's sugar and fresh blueberries.

NOTE

PARVE VARIATION

For a parve variation, substitute frozen and fresh
strawberries and parve
vanilla ice cream.

WATERMELON SORBET

My sister is an overachiever. Whenever she does any-thing, she won't stop short of it being the best. When she was appointed in charge of desserts one Pesach, not only did she bake, but she created everything in abundance — including this watermelon sorbet. She made tubs and tubs of it, and we were licking our spoons until Shavuos. This is an adapted version. (I don't want her to say that I didn't get it right!)

YIELD 8 SERVINGS

1¼ CUP	**SUGAR**
½ CUP	**WATER**
¼ CUP	**LEMON JUICE**
½ CUP	**ORANGE JUICE**
3 CUPS	**WATERMELON PURÉE***

* To prepare the purée, cut a watermelon into chunks and remove all the seeds. Puree in a food processor.

1 In a small saucepan, cook the sugar, water, and juices together, stirring occasionally, until sugar is fully dis-solved. Chill.

2 Measure 3 cups of watermelon puree and combine with the chilled syrup. Freeze the entire mixture in a 9x13-inch pan. When sorbet is fully frozen, cut into chunks. Working in batches, blend the chunks in the food processor quickly, until the mixture is smooth. Return to the pan and re-freeze. Repeat the blending process one more time and allow to freeze fully before serving.

CHOCOLATE ROCKY ROAD ICE CREAM

PARVE

YIELD 1 QUART

3	**EGGS,** SEPARATED
⅓ CUP	**SUGAR**
2 (3½oz) BARS	**GOOD-QUALITY PARVE CHOCOLATE**
1 8oz CONTAINER	**NON-DAIRY WHIPPED TOPPING**
¾ CUP	**BLANCHED SLIVERED ALMONDS,** TOASTED
¾ CUP	**MINI MARSHMALLOWS**

Ice cream is addictive. Did you ever meet a kid who can pass an ice cream parlor and not beg for some? Never mind the kids — one of my friends in Israel went out and bought three cartons of Ben and Jerry's ice cream "to taste" in honor of Shabbos when it received a chalav yisrael hechsher. She and her husband ate one pint after kiddush on Shabbos morning, one after the fish, one after the eggs, then took a walk around the block before ending their ice cream madness by finally eating the cholent. Ice cream is one addiction we never outgrow.

1 Beat egg whites until stiff. Gradually add the sugar and continue beating until stiff peaks form. Set aside.

2 Chop the chocolate into pieces and melt over a double boiler or in the microwave (34-45 seconds on high). Leave some of the pieces semi-melted, so you'll have some chocolate chunks in the ice cream. Let cool slightly.

3 Using a fork, mix the egg yolks with the cooled chocolate until thoroughly combined. Set aside.

4 Beat the whipped topping until stiff. Add the chocolate/egg mixture, and continue mixing until it is uniform in color. Fold in the whites, toasted almonds, and mini marshmallows. Pour into 6-cup container. Freeze until firm.

BUBBLE GUM ICE CREAM

PARVE

This dessert is certain to make you the most popular mother, aunt, or grandmother on the block.

1   Defrost ice cream slightly. Mix gell powder into the vanilla ice cream until thoroughly combined and ice cream turns a light pink color. Gently fold in the gumballs. Freeze.

2   This recipe works best with homemade vanilla ice cream, as it tends to be much softer than the store-bought variety.

YIELD 1 QUART

1 QUART	**PARVE VANILLA ICE CREAM**
3 TBSP	**TROPICAL PUNCH-FLAVORED GELL DESSERT POWDER**
30	**COLORFUL MINI GUMBALLS**

PECAN CHOCOLATE ICE CREAM ROLL

I served pecan ice cream one Shabbos when my friend Chani was eating over. She asked for the recipe and made the ice cream a few weeks later. The same day, she was also preparing a chocolate roll. On a whim, she decided that they go together. I think so too.

YIELD 10-12 SERVINGS

CHOCOLATE ROLL CAKE

7	**EGGS,** SEPARATED
7 TBSP	**SUGAR**
4 TBSP	**FLOUR**
4 TBSP	**COCOA**
1 TBSP	**VANILLA SUGAR**
•	**CONFECTIONER'S SUGAR,** FOR DUSTING

PECAN ICE CREAM

3	**EGGS,** SEPARATED
⅓ CUP	**SUGAR**
2 TBSP	**MAPLE SYRUP**
1 8oz CONTAINER	**NON-DAIRY WHIPPED TOPPING**
½ CUP	**GLAZED PECANS,** COARSELY CHOPPED

1   Preheat oven to 350°F.

2   Beat the egg whites until foamy. Gradually add the sugar and beat until stiff peaks form. Reduce speed to low and add the yolks, flour, cocoa, and vanilla sugar.

3   Spread mixture evenly on a baking sheet lined with parchment paper. Bake for 18 minutes.

4   Liberally sprinkle a kitchen towel with confectioner's sugar. Invert the cake onto the towel. Carefully peel off the parchment paper and roll up with the towel, jellyroll style. Set aside and allow to cool.

5   To prepare the pecan ice cream, beat the egg whites with sugar until stiff peaks form. Set aside.

6   Using a fork, combine the egg yolks and maple syrup. Beat the whipped topping until stiff. Add the egg yolk mixture and mix until thoroughly combined. Fold in the beaten whites. Add the chopped pecans.

7   To assemble, gently unroll the cake. Spread ¾ of the ice cream over the entire surface and roll up, jellyroll style. Spread the remaining ice cream over the cake. Garnish with additional pecans. Serve frozen.

BROWNIE ICE CREAM SANDWICHES

DAIRY OR PARVE

YIELD 20-24 COOKIES DEPENDING ON SIZE

1 CUP (2 STICKS)	MARGARINE
½ CUP	SUGAR
2	EGGS
1 TSP	VANILLA EXTRACT
⅔ CUP	COCOA
3¼ CUPS	FLOUR
½ TSP	SALT
½ TSP	BAKING POWDER
1 GALLON	ICE CREAM, DAIRY OR PARVE, FLAVOR OF YOUR CHOICE

Seudah Shelishit (the third Shabbos meal) in sleepaway camp was one of my favorite times of the week. We ate and sang songs until the stars came out and it was time for Havdalah. One of the highlights was the ice cream sandwich that was served for dessert. During my first summer, I quickly learned to never leave the table when the ice cream sandwiches were being served. When a girl did get up from the table, leaving her wrapped ice cream sandwich on her plate, swift and experienced tricksters quickly unwrapped the sandwich, replace the ice cream with sour cream and proceeded to close the wrapper so well that no one would be the wiser. I can't remember who the girl was who tasted a sour cream sandwich that Shabbos, but I do remember her reaction.

Some may think this story borders on cruelty and shouldn't be repeated. I included it because I feel it teaches us an important lesson: never let good things out of your sight!

1   Preheat oven to 350°F.

2   In the bowl of a mixer, cream the margarine and sugar. Add the eggs, vanilla, and cocoa. In a separate bowl, combine the flour, salt, and baking powder. Gradually add the flour mixture to the bowl and combine until smooth. Place dough into a plastic bag and refrigerate for a minimum of one hour.   ▶

3. Roll out cookie dough on a floured surface until it is ⅛-¼-inch thick. You may need to use additional flour to keep dough from sticking. (Don't worry about the flour on the dark cookie. It disappears when it bakes.) With a cookie cutter, cut desired shapes and place on baking sheet lined with parchment paper.

4. Bake for 8-11 minutes until edges are firm and the centers are slightly soft and puffed. Let cool.

5. To assemble, slightly defrost the ice cream, spread over a baking sheet lined with parchment paper, and re-freeze. Using the same cookie cutter, cut out ice cream shapes. Place between 2 cookies and freeze.

NOTE

SERVING IDEAS

Cut cookies into large flower shapes. Serve one cookie with a scoop of ice cream and warm fudge sauce on top.

Some find it easier to serve two cookies with a scoop of ice cream in between, so that guests can use a spoon, lift off the top cookie, eat the ice cream, and then eat the cookie without holding the sandwich in their hands.

ALMOND ICE CREAM CUPS

YIELD 8-10 COOKIE CUPS

¼ CUP (½ STICK)	**MARGARINE**
½ CUP	**NON-DAIRY WHIPPED TOPPING**
⅛ TSP	**VANILLA EXTRACT**
¾ CUP	**GROUND ALMONDS**
⅔ CUP	**SUGAR**
2 (HEAPING) TBSP	**FLOUR**

These make a really beautiful presentation without much work. You might need some practice to get the cookie baked just right. Your oven temperature can make all the difference. If it's too low, your cookie won't shape. If it's too hot, your overbaked cookie will crack. Once you learn how long these need to bake in your oven, they are really easy to make.

1   In a small saucepan, over medium-low heat, melt the margarine and whipped topping. Remove from heat and stir in the vanilla. Add remaining ingredients and mix well. Refrigerate until thoroughly chilled. (Best if left overnight and can be left in the refrigerator for up to 4 days.)

2   Preheat oven to 350°F. Stir the batter. Drop 1 Tablespoon of batter onto a baking sheet lined with parchment paper (do not place more than 2 Tablespoons at a time on a sheet).

3   Bake for 8-11 minutes until cookies spread and turn honey brown. Remove pan and let cool for 1 minute.

4   Remove cookie and place over the bottom of an upside-down ramekin or small bowl. Press cookie and allow sides to bend to the contours of the bowl or ramekin. Let harden. Repeat with remaining batter.

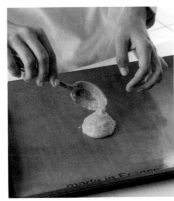

5 If the cookie is too brittle to bend, return to oven for one minute, as the heat will allow it to soften. If the cookie is too soft and is tearing, allow it to cool longer. If cooling does not work, the cookie may be underbaked and needs more time in the oven.

6 To store, place a piece of parchment paper or plastic bag between the layers of cookies. Can be stored at room temperature or frozen to prevent cup shape from sagging.

7 Serve with fruit or ice cream inside.

BROWNIE BITS ICE CREAM

YIELD 2 QUARTS

BROWNIE BATTER

1 CUP	SUGAR
½ CUP	FLOUR
½ TSP	BAKING POWDER
⅓ CUP	COCOA
PINCH	SALT
2	EGGS
⅓ CUP	OIL

BASIC ICE CREAM

4	EGGS, SEPARATED
½ CUP	SUGAR
2 8oz CONTAINERS	NON-DAIRY WHIPPED TOPPING
1 TBSP	VANILLA SUGAR

If you want to try these brownies on their own, double the recipe and bake for 45-50 minutes.

1 Preheat the oven to 350°F.

2 In a large bowl, combine the sugar, flour, baking powder, cocoa, and salt. Use a fork to mix in the eggs and oil. Place the batter into 9x13-inch pan. Bake for 30-40 minutes. When still warm, cut into little cubes, about the size of a postage stamp or smaller.

3 To prepare the ice cream, beat the egg whites and gradually add the sugar until stiff peaks form. Refrigerate.

4 Beat whipped topping until light and fluffy. Add the yolks and vanilla and beat to combine well. Fold the egg whites into this batter. Fold in the brownie bits, incorporating thoroughly. Freeze in a 9x13-inch pan or 2-quart plastic container.

PECANS & KISSES

7 oz	**PECANS**
7 oz	**MERINGUE KISSES**
2 8oz CONTAINER	**NON-DAIRY WHIPPED TOPPING**

This simple recipe is a solution for those who like home-made ice cream but prefer to avoid raw eggs. It's as simple as could be and quite sweet, so serve small portions.

1   Chop the pecans and set aside. Place the meringues into a plastic bag, and with a rolling pin, roll over meringues to crush the kisses (don't crush to dust; you want to retain small chunks). Beat the whipped topping until high and fluffy. Fold in the crushed pecans and meringue kisses.

2   Freeze in individual silicone molds or a loaf pan. Remove from freezer, unmold or cut slices just before serving.

CHOCOLATE MOUSSE WITH PEAR CHIPS

YIELD 8-10 SERVINGS

8	**EGGS,** SEPARATED
12 oz	**BITTERSWEET CHOCOLATE** (NOT BAKING)
1 TSP	**INSTANT COFFEE GRANULES,** DISSOLVED IN 3 TBSP BOILING WATER
¼ CUP	**SWEET RED WINE**

PEAR CHIPS

2	**FIRM PEARS**
1 CUP	**SUGAR**

Thanks to my mother-in-law for this classic family favorite.

1 In a mixer, whip the egg whites until stiff peaks form.

2 Over a double boiler, melt the chocolate with the coffee. Beat egg yolks, with a fork and quickly add to double boiler, mixing well. Add the red wine. Remove from heat.

3 Fold in the egg whites until combined. Place in individual cups for serving. Refrigerate.

4 To prepare pear chips, preheat oven to 325°F.

5 Thinly slice the pears and lightly coat each side with sugar. Place the pear slices in a single layer on a baking sheet lined with parchment paper. Bake for 15-20 minutes. Turn the pears over and bake for an additional 15-20 minutes. Turn off the oven and leave the pears in the oven to cool and dry.

6 Before serving, garnish mousse with chocolate shavings and caramelized pear chips.

TRI-COLOR FRUIT PURÉE

YIELD 3 CUPS
BASIC APPLESAUCE

APPLESAUCE

6	**APPLES** (ANY KIND BUT PREFERABLY GREEN)
1 CUP	**BOILING WATER**
3 TBSP	**LEMON JUICE,** FROM ONE LEMON
1 TBSP	**VANILLA SUGAR**
6-7 TBSP	**SUGAR**

STRAWBERRY VARIATION

1½ CUPS	**STRAWBERRIES,** FRESH OR FROZEN

KIWI VARIATION

3-4	**KIWIS,** PEELED

PINEAPPLE VARIATION

2 CUPS	**FRESH PINEAPPLE,** CUT INTO CHUNKS

Most dessert lovers like to indulge in chocolate treats, mousses, crisps topped with ice cream, and velvety cakes. Then there are those who prefer simpler sweet endings like applesauce and fruit compotes. I never considered those items fitting desserts, and for years, ignored the homemade applesauce on my mother-in-law's dessert table. Then one day she served two colors of sauce together, and it spoke to me. I tasted it, and it was purely and simply divine. I can't say I prefer it over chocolate cake, but I definitely joined the crowd that's capable of digging into a tub of … applesauce.

1   Peel, core and cut the apples into large chunks. Place the apple chunks into a sauce pot and pour boiling water over them. Sprinkle with lemon juice and sugars and return to a boil. Lower heat to medium and cook until the apples are completely soft, stirring occasionally. Turn off the heat and let apples cool. Use an immersion blender or food processor to blend the cooled apples with the cooking water.

2   Strawberry/apple variation: Add 1½ cups of strawberries to the pot. Fresh strawberries should be added with the apples. Frozen strawberries should be added halfway through the cooking process.

3   Kiwi/apple variation: Blend 3 or 4 kiwis until smooth. Add them to the blended applesauce.

4   Pineapple/apple variation: Add chunks of fresh pineapple to the pot while cooking.

NOTE

Cooking time varies, depending on the size of the pot and variety of apple, so keep an eye on the apples as they cook and test for doneness.

INDEX

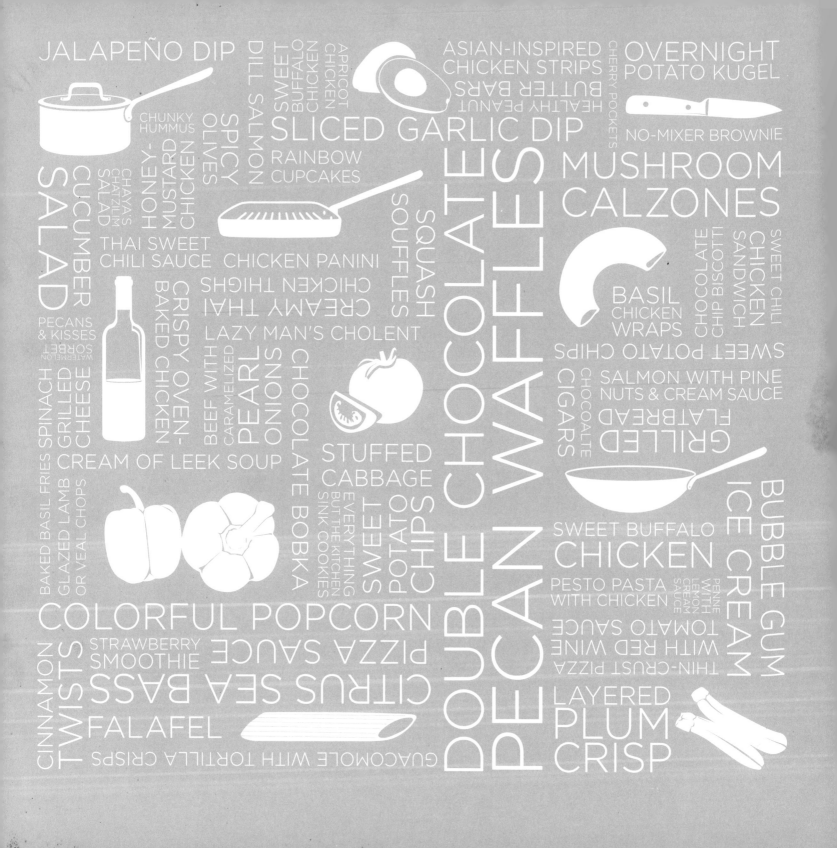